HORROR ADDICTS GUIDE TO LIFE

Horror Addicts Guide to Life

Copyright © 2015 HorrorAddicts.net

Printed in the United States of America.
Edited by David Watson
Cover art: Carmen Masloski
Publisher: HorrorAddicts.net
        Emerian Rich
        HorrorAddicts@gmail.com

ISBN: 978-1508772521

www.horroraddicts.net

HORROR ADDICTS GUIDE TO LIFE

Edited by David Watson

contents

horror reading

horror music

horror party planning

horror fashion

from the editor

Right about the time I came on staff at HorrorAddicts.net, I heard of a book called *Encyclopedia Gotthica* by Lisa Ladouceur. This book was all about the goth lifestyle. When I heard about it, I thought, "What a cool idea for a book." I grew up in a small town and didn't know what a goth was until I was twenty-one and stumbled into a goth dance at a comic convention. In all honesty, I still don't know a lot about goths but the more I learn, the more I realize I'm a goth at heart. I may not dress like one, but I have a lot of the same interests. That being said, I can't consider myself goth, but I can call myself a horror addict.

This is why I got interested in the HorrorAddicts.net podcast. I heard the promo for it on The Pod Of Horror podcast and it appealed to me. The hostess, Emerian Rich, presented her podcast as a program that promotes the horror lifestyle and she tried to include fashion, movies, books, games, conventions, decorating for Halloween, and everything else you could think of. I loved the show from the first time I heard it and was ecstatic when she invited me to be a part of the staff.

Ever since I can remember, I loved the horror genre. I was drawn to any book that had a monster on it. My favorite cartoons were the ones with monsters and ghosts in them like *Casper, The Drac Pack, The Groovie Ghoulies, Godzilla,* and *Scooby Doo.* When I made up games to play, there were always monsters in them and when I was little I always tried to stay up late to see *Creature Feature* on late night TV.

As I got older, I read horror film magazines, discovered the works of Stephen King and several other horror authors, and went to R-rated horror films in the theatre as soon as I was old enough.

People told me as a teenager that I would grow out of my love of horror, but I never did. I still love the horror genre in all its forms.

I've been a horror addict all my life and I think horror addicts look at the world in a different way, which is why we need a *Horror Addicts Guide to Life*. To illustrate my point, back in August of 2011 I wrote a post on World Goth Day. This day was started to pay homage to Sophie Lancaster, a girl in the United Kingdom who was brutally killed by a group of people for being goth. Writing that blog post really made me sad. Sophie was killed just because a group of kids didn't like that she was different. Fellow HorrorAddicts.net staff member and UK resident, Ed Pope, commented on the post saying he was happy we mentioned it on the blog. He remembered the story and it sickened him. I commented back that it was a hard post to write. I can watch the goriest movie and it wouldn't bother me, but true life horror in the form of an innocent girl being tortured like that deeply disturbed me. Ed said that those who have a firm grasp of fictional horror, process real life horrors in a way that makes it even more disturbing.

Horror fans look at the world in a different way and hopefully this guide will give a glimpse as to how horror fans look at life. Horror isn't an interest, it's a lifestyle, and in this book you will find several articles by people that feel the same way. If you don't understand why people love the horror genre, this book will show you why some of us make horror a lifestyle. If you're already a lover of all things horror then you are going to love this book.

David Watson, *Editor*

what is a horror addict?

nightshade welcomes You

What is a horror addict? Before I answer that I should introduce myself, my name is Nightshade Traxler, and I'm the star of this book. My name may not be on the cover, but my picture is and make no mistake about it, this book is mine.

What is a horror addict? Our kin over at HorrorAddicts.net defines it as, "A person who is physiologically or psychologically dependent on items depicting macabre events."

I'm the ultimate horror addict and I'm the perfect person to guide you through this book. You don't believe me? Well, let me tell you about myself. I grew up in a big spooky house, the kind everyone in the neighborhood whispers about. You probably have one like it in your neighborhood. My mom sang in a band that did songs about zombies and vampires, while my dad wrote horror novels. Or at least that's what I think they did, I was a little suspicious about the body-shaped packages coming in and out of the basement. Anyway, they were different, some would say odd. Every day in my house was Halloween and that inspired me to be a life-long horror fan.

I'm always the first in line to see new horror movies and I'm forever in search of a good horror novel. I wear black so I can let my horror flag fly. Some people may run *from* a scary looking house, but I like to run *toward* it. I love to be scared. Screaming makes me feel alive and I love to scare people as much as I love to get scared.

Horror is fun for me because it's all about emotion and it's a more acceptable way to deal with the drama in our lives. Screaming about vampires sucking blood from helpless victims can be a metaphor for several different real life horrors. Plus, vampires are just plain cool. Horror addicts aren't disturbed people. We love a thrill and we believe you can find beauty in the darkest places.

I'll be your guide on this ghoulish adventure through the macabre landscape that is: being a horror addict in today's day and age. In this first section, there are a couple of articles that should explain why us addicts love horror. We all have our reasons to love the genre and we all find different things scary. Personally, I find waiting in line at the grocery store scary and because I'm a really nice person, and want other people to be scared with me, I bring some fake blood along. While I'm in line I put the blood on my arm, and scream out, "There are zombies loose in the store and they bit me!" I then proceed to act like I'm undead and watch the customers in front of me leave the store in terror. This is also a good way to make the wait in line a lot shorter.

what is horror?

by David Watson

Not long ago, I got an email from an author who was upset with me because I talked about one of her books on the HorrorAddicts.net blog and I said her writing combined horror and mystery. In her email, she said she doesn't write horror. She continued to say, horror is all about blood and guts and shocking people and she doesn't do that. She wanted to make it clear, what she writes is paranormal mystery. I replied to her that to me, paranormal falls into the horror genre and horror can be a lot of different things, not just blood and guts.

This lady's email really got me thinking. What is horror? I asked people in the HorrorAddicts.net Facebook group and several people responded. Chantal Boudreau, who you will find in this anthology, said, "Horror is about a lot more than gore." The other responses on what horror is, said it's a broad topic that can be a lot of different things, but basically horror is anything that scares you.

So even though one author sees paranormal mystery as not being horror, other people say paranormal does fit into the horror genre. Paranormal includes anything that doesn't have a scientific explanation such as ghosts, psychic powers, or extrasensory perception. People are scared of what they do not understand, and since paranormal deals with the unknown, I think it's horror.

I would even go a little farther with this and say there are a lot of different sub genres to horror. Comedies such as *The Addams Family* or *The Munsters* fit into the horror genre. A lot of science fiction can also be classified as horror such as *Alien* or *The*

Terminator. For me personally, I think hospitals can be scary places, so a show like *ER* can fit into the horror category for me. Even police dramas such as *Criminal Minds* or *The Following* can be horror because these shows deal with serial killers and that definitely fills most people with a sense of fear.

To me, even though I would consider the *Friday the 13th* movies—which I never liked—and *The Nightmare On Elm Street* movies—which I loved—horror, I didn't find them very scary. So to me, something doesn't have to be scary to be considered horror. As I've gotten older I find movies don't scare me anymore, but books still do. That being said, I still enjoy watching horror movies, but I look at them as more funny than scary. I would still throw them into the horror category, though.

So to me, horror just describes something that is dark, different, or misunderstood, not necessarily shocking or scary. What do you consider horror? What scares you? Do you consider something horror if it doesn't scare you? Can scary sounding music fit into the horror genre? Also, what makes you love horror? Email us at <u>horroraddicts@gmail.com</u> and let us know.

what is horrifying to me?

by Ron Vitale

I woke up startled from a noise. It was the middle of the night and I had been sleeping. I opened my eyes and floated between consciousness and sleep, my mind reeling. Still in bed, I saw lights in the hallway. The lights appeared to dance in the air and I heard an odd noise that rushed toward me. The sound, distant yet constant, appeared to be coming from the strange lights levitating in my hallway. My teenage body froze in fear. The lights grew in size, moving closer to my doorway as they increased in intensity. I tried to move again and could not. Trapped in pure horror, I remained paralyzed and could not speak and I tried thinking but my brain refused to work. The rumbling noise faded and the lights faded back.

And then I knew it, a ghost or an angel had come to visit me. Torn between which it might be, I desperately pushed aside the thought that a ghost had come to haunt me and take my soul. In my compromised state, an angel seemed the better option. But this ethereal being sounded more like Gabriel coming with his sword to wreak havoc on the unjust than to help a poor soul like me. As the rumbling sound increased in volume, shaking the apartment, the lights flared up, angry and brilliantly white. They floated toward the door and I begged them to not hurt me. The horror of my predicament left me powerless. The angel of death had come for me and instead of being asleep as it had intended, I saw my last few minutes on this Earth before being taken. I was dragged into the chute of hell, to writhe with the rest of the unfortunate souls who had not done God's will. I would suffer for all eternity, cast

5

aside and adrift from the light, only to be in utter darkness and fear—forever.

I cannot tell you how many minutes my run-in with the angel of death lasted, but I can tell you how I woke from it. Having heard the sound again, my sleepy brain began to put two and two together. The "roar" and "rumble" were trucks and cars passing by our apartment. The sound of their passing was echoing off a wall and coming in through the bathroom window. Similarly, I then realized that the light from their headlights was reflecting off the bathroom mirror and then onto the full length hallway mirror creating the illusion of floating balls of light. A logical answer for my other worldly experience was simply that I had been in a dream state and a large truck rumbled by. I wasn't quite awake and saw the lights, thinking they were some spirits coming to get me. When you're fifteen years old and have an active imagination, that's all it took to instill dreadful horror into me.

But what is horror? Truly, what does it mean? For our edification, I looked it up on Wikipedia and learned that horror is defined as:

Horror: noun
1. an overwhelming and painful feeling caused by something frightfully shocking, terrifying, or revolting; a shuddering fear: to shrink back from a mutilated corpse in horror.

Now that we know what horror is defined as, I'd like to expound a bit on what horror means to me. I'll be honest: I'm a scaredy cat. It doesn't take much to frighten me, but there is power in horror. I'd like to propose that the anticipation of an event or action is so much more powerful and horrifying than any monster Hollywood can put on the big screen. I love CGI, but it pales in comparison to my imagination.

A few examples. Remember, the movie *Jaws*? There's a scene in the beginning in which a young woman is swimming at night. She feels a tug at her leg and a confused look crosses her face. Then it happens again and she's pulled under the water. She's scared, it's dark, you can't see much and then she's dragged around and pulled under. Many minutes go by in the film until you actually see the shark. Granted, with the limited technology at the time, the shark isn't much to look at. In 2015, who would be afraid of that mechanical monstrosity? But re-watch the film and take in what Spielberg does to build suspense and fear. Granted, *Jaws* is not a horror film, but, as a little kid, it was my first understanding of how powerful my imagination could be.

A few years later, *Alien* came out and I was only eight at the time, so I didn't get to see the movie until it was on video a few years later. But I'll never forget the stomach-bursting scene and Ridley Scott's use of the camera. How many long, smoking corridors does he bring us down as the crew searches for the creature? How many times do you think it's going to pop out and instead it's a cat or nothing? Building that suspense and then, when you least expect it, the creature would come out and scare the crap out of my pre-teen self.

And my third example will be a controversial one. I've learned that there's a split camp on this one. I'll break the argument down as such:

I saw *The Blair Witch Project* before all the hype. My brother waited until the movie had been blown up into being something that would scare God Herself. There's a scene at the end (I apologize for the spoiler but the film came out in 1999 so stop reading this if you haven't seen it) in which Mike is standing facing a wall. You know something's there (the witch creature thingy) and Heather falls down and the camera is knocked on its side. There's screams and the camera fades out. Boom. The End. Now I saw the film, thought it was good and came home and that night I had nightmares that freaked the hell out of me. Why?

I could not stop replaying the ending of the movie in my head: Mike is standing in the corner, hunched a bit like he's a little boy, immobile and trapped by the witch. She/it is there in the room waiting to get Heather. With the darkened, grainy video, you don't see much. I didn't need to, but my imagination filled in the rest. In my dream, I replayed that ending scene and was horrified at the potential for evil in that room. My psyche can dredge up the most imaginative creatures, places or events that will tear at my mind, enabling me to live in that moment. I had not been more terrified and frightened from a movie's ending in a long time.

My brother laughed at me. "Dude, there's a guy standing in front of a wall. The bitch trips and drops the camera and then she screams and the camera fades. What's up with that?"

I understand his point. I do. But, for me, true horror isn't what we see on the screen or read on the page. It's the anticipation, the implied horror that can take your feeble human mind and break you down into the puny little kid you once were—afraid of lights dancing in the hallway in the middle of night.

I would argue that the best horror masterpieces embrace that human weakness of ours: We want to know and put explanations to the unknowable. An odd noise or sight: We will think it's a ghost, a creature or a UFO. And to me, finding the intersection between what we think we know and try to anticipate what we know is the true horror. It's hearing the odd noise in the middle of the night in a darkened house. Is it the house settling or is someone there, waiting for you?

By no means am I saying that my definition of horror is the "right" one. No, that's not true at all. But I would ask that if you are, like my brother, loving the exploding guts and mindless zombies eating the intestines of hapless teenagers on the screen or in books, I'd recommend trying a different type of horror. Explore what you can't see and let your imagination fill in the gaps. I wonder: Will what you dream up be more horrifying? There's only one way to find out…

horror lifestyle

nightshade on lifestyle

The horror lifestyle is something I probably don't have to explain to most of you. Personally, one of the ways I live the horror lifestyle is by making my home look as scary as possible. Every day is Halloween at Nightshade's abode and when victims...I mean visitors come 'round, I'm ready to have some fun.

For instance, when a salesman comes to my door I like to put the vampire fangs in, a cape on, and act like everything is normal. If they talk to me too long I start sniffing the air and say, "Mmm your blood smells wonderful, can I have a little taste?" Then I hit him with an intense stare that lets him know I mean business. Needless to say, salespeople have learned to avoid my home. Best solicitor repellent on the market is acting crazy or murderous. Hehee.

Our first section is about the horror lifestyle. These people make horror a part of their everyday lives. Some have gothic tea parties and others like to hang out in graveyards. As fellow horror addicts, we don't judge them because we understand them on an intimate level. So go on addicts, express your dark passion.

Why I hang out in Graveyards

by Mimi A. Williams

For most people, graveyards are places they choose not to visit unless they absolutely, positively can't avoid it. That either means that someone close to them has passed away, or they themselves have. But I have a slightly different take on things: I find graveyards to be very inspiring.

As a writer, I find inspiration in a lot of places, but what appeals to me about old graveyards (the older, the better!) is that they are filled with stories waiting to be told—or to be imagined. My former writing partner and I used to spend a lot of time wandering around two of the oldest graveyards in our city. We found the environment was not only useful because it was quiet, but we found being surrounded by death makes you look at life in a new way. We even found things to laugh about! For example, meaning absolutely no disrespect, what would you think upon discovering a tombstone with the name Studness on it?

Graveyards are great sources for names as well. Many of my characters names have been uncovered on tombstones, wholly or in part. I find names of towns I've never heard of that go into a book of story notes I keep. I also find pieces of history. In one tiny family cemetery down in the southern part of Utah, I noted how several members of one family ranging in ages from thirteen months up to thirty-four years, had all passed away within weeks of each other. Clearly this was some sort of epidemic that hit their family, and perhaps the wider community (such as it was) at

14

the time. My mind immediately went to the idea of being one of the survivors, or worse, of being the only survivor. From that point on, a new story began to take shape in my mind and it is now lined up (behind a few others) waiting for me to work on.

The headstones themselves tell a remarkable story. The large, ornate mausoleums stand side by side with the traditional arched grave markers. To me it's an interesting contrast, and a little bit ironic. No matter how much money you had in life, once you're gone, you can't tell by the bones who belonged in which location. But there are those who insist on leaving a lasting mark, even though eventually, no one will remain to appreciate who lies within nor what his or her net worth once was.

Cemeteries also force us to confront our own mortality. Little else speaks to us of death the way a bunch of dead bodies can! For many people the idea of death is a frightening one. Sometimes it's the fear of the unknown. Sometimes it's a fear of some form of eternal punishment. I don't want to get into a philosophical or religious discussion here, but I will say, I don't find anything frightening about being dead. How could it possibly be worse than the hell we humans have created in this life? For my part, I'm comfortable with the thought of death because it truly is the great equalizer. We all end up in the same place (more or less) dealing with the same circumstances. Death is far less frightening than the dentist I went to as a child—that's for sure.

The old Salt Lake City cemetery is located on the north end of the city, up in the foothills. I often wonder if there were to be an earthquake, if we would see some of our dearly departed once again. My favorite cemetery here, however, is Mount Olivet located near the University of Utah. Lovely, large trees, a man-made stream that meanders through the location, and a resident herd of deer make this place idyllic. There is a section where many members of the Greek community are buried which is very near the Jewish section of the grounds. The marble mausoleums are there, and sculptures of angels and young girls as well. Many members of the various Masonic fraternities are buried here, and they even have their own amphitheater for holding services. It's a lovely place to sit and write as well.

At <u>Facebook.com/mimiloveshorror</u>, I have a collection of photos taken at Mount Olivet, including one of Studness, and a few others I have enjoyed for various reasons. If you happen to be in Utah, I encourage you to stop by and visit. I think you'll find, as I have, that hanging out in cemeteries can be a very life-affirming and inspiring way to spend some time.☻

Goths in the workplace

by Emerian Rich

Do goth or alternative lifestyle employees have to work harder than the norms in the modern workplace? I am a gloom cookie, a mistress of the dark, a "goth" as the norms call us. I wear black clothes, color my hair, and sport elaborate makeup. I've worked for employers that don't care what I wear and ones that have dress codes that make me alter or tone down my look, but at the core I am still me and I will be me, whether they like it or not. Those of us who live alternative lives—whether you be a goth, lolita, punk, gay, or have an uncommon religion—are different. We see things differently. We process things differently and have different answers to mainstream questions. Some of us hide or disguise our differences so we can have a simpler life, but in the end, we are different and you have to be a pretty good magician to hide it at all times, even in the workplace.

I don't have to tell you that the norm perception of us is bad. Apparently we are evil, devil worshiping, spell casting, curse making, sexually perverse, murderous fiends who will stop at nothing to "turn" them (fill in the blank) goth, gay, or evil. God forbid you fall into two or three of these different alternative categories. To them, a gay male, goth, pagan, has one intent: To corrupt their way of life and turn their sons into flaming voodoo priests! I'm not going to tackle how we change that impression in this post, that is so much bigger than ourselves. However, given that the impression of the general public is this, do we have to work harder in the workplace to prove our usefulness? To earn respect, do we have to be better, faster, and sharper than the norms?

17

I think we do. Because not only do they think we are "weird", they also believe that we spend our work hours thinking "weird things." It doesn't matter that your cube mate is obsessed with her pet tabby cat wearing sweater sets and has pictures of the feline plastering her side of the cube. No, that is an acceptable hobby. Yet, if we mention just once about a concert, book, or a movie we like, they instantly place us in the antagonist position. I can hear the conversations by the water cooler.

"Omg... she said she just LOVES the *Saw* movies. What do you think her house looks like? Do you think she has meat hooks and table saws? Do you think she's going to kill us all?"

Something that goes along with their perception of us is that we are lazy or try to get out of work. You know, because we need time to plot our destruction of their lives. Do you feel like, as a goth in the workplace, you are treated unfairly or held to a higher standard? Or perhaps judged more harshly because of your outward appearance or special interests? Do you find that you have to work harder for respect when your norm co-worker is constantly late and plays Facebook games all day but earns kudos easily? Do you think the way you dress or things you enjoy on your off-time hinder you from getting raises, promotions, or special incentives?

I once worked for a company where I was the token goth. I was the person they liked to put on the forefront to show others how diverse they were, but even known as the diversity proof, the stereotypes didn't end. The fact is, unless you are willing to abandon your look or personality completely, you will be discriminated against. Until our general populace starts to really accept people's differences in truth—

not just in word—we will have to continue to wear down the prejudices that plague people of our kind.

I've worked with people who thought my dress code had something to do with my religion and they were shocked when I handed out holiday candy. Hmm...do all Catholics wear pink? Not really, so why would all people who wear black be Satanists? It's a color people! Just saying. A lot of these stereotypes are not even logical.

I've been blamed for bad business deals because I like the number thirteen and good friends (or not so good friends it turns out) have accused me of putting curses on them. I'm sorry, but I don't have time to plot against you. If I had the ability to cast voodoo magic, I would definitely use that power to improve MY situation in life, not bring yours down. Here's an interesting thought: If the majority of the norm public doesn't believe magic or spell casting is real, why do they assume we can wield it against them?

I've worked for good people too. Ones that understood or at least try to allow for my way of life, but these are not common. Why? What's going to happen if you get close to a goth? I have to admit, there is a slim chance of getting black eyeliner on you, but beyond that, we are good people. Sure, there are the bad apples, just like any set of people, but for the most part we are kind, imaginative, interesting people and you are missing out on some terrific friendships.

I pride myself on being good at my job. No matter what the task is, I take time management and execution very seriously. I am a perfectionist and list maker and I rarely slack off. I work hard and I expect to be treated kindly and respected by my co-workers and managers. For these reasons, I have been able to earn respect at several companies by showing what I can do, but it wasn't easy. If I was the cookie cutter worker, would I have more opportunity for advancement sooner? Who knows. It feels like it. Being a goth in the workplace almost feels like being on probation from day one. Guilty until proven innocent.

Because we are constantly trying to break down the stereotypes and work harder to prove we are not flakes or idiots, do alternative lifestyle people in the mainstream workforce have more stress in their lives? Do you find yourself getting sick more than others do or feeling exhausted at keeping up the charade? How long is the life expectancy of a goth in the modern office? I bet that's one they haven't tested! Why? Because we may melt in the light of day?

I've been very sarcastic in this piece, but I really want to know. I'm interested in your view on this subject. How do you feel you are discriminated against in your office? How have you dealt with the hurdles you've faced? If you are not a goth, and are scared to get to know us, why? What fears can we break down for you? What makes you so scared? If you have feedback for me, please email horroraddicts@gmail.com.

♥

bedtime...
horror addicts style

by Chantal Boudreau

Be it nightmares, night terrors or just a fear of the dark, there is something essentially scary about bedtime. For that very reason you'll find an assortment of ways people attempt to counter that fear: soothing lullabies, protective prayers, gentle fairy tales, soft night lights, and dream-catchers, all used in an attempt to fend off the frightful. What is it exactly that makes bedtime so scary?

Better yet, why would we as horror addicts fight that fright?

Well, I for one feel we should be looking to embrace the fear rather than struggling to chase it away. For someone who finds the terrifying appealing, bedtime presents the opportunity to intensify the fun. Allow me to share a few suggestions that can make bedtime all the more frightful.

Ghoulish Bedtime Stories:

Are *Goodnight Moon* and *The Velveteen Rabbit* too tame for your blood? Would you rather read something that would be more likely to inspire nightmares? Alvin Schwartz's *Scary Stories to Tell in the Dark*, Yolen and Murphy's *Creepy Monsters, Sleepy Monsters*, or Snow and Hunters' *Hugging Your Pillow Tight* are bedtime stories intended to add some screams to your dreams. If those won't do, crack open some classic Poe or the more modern *Dream Walkers and Nightmare Stalkers* from Horrified Press— bedtime stories at their scariest.

21

Scary Apparel:

Some folks have their fuzzy slippers and teddy bear PJs to wear to bed, but those are hardly the kind of sleepwear appropriate for a horror addict. For something with more scare flair, Thinkgeek.com and Zombiegift.com offer zombie slippers and pajamas. CafePress.com lists a variety of horror-themed nightwear, from "Come to Freddy" nighties to Lovecraftian footy long johns (I kid you not.) You can even find yourself a startling plushy to cling to at night at thingsthatgoboo.com. I love their Teddy Scares Bears and Skelanimals.

Terrifying Bedding:

Snuggling down in your cuddly blanky or down-filled duvet may be good for some, but I prefer my comforters not so comforting. To add some chill to your sheets without cranking up the air conditioner, how about these possibilities: Zombiegift.com has an assortment of walking dead fleece blankets and zombie girl and boy pillows. Horrordecor.net offers an amazing selection of gloomy pillowcases, blankets and sheets—their *Saw* Jigsaw pillow rocks. Just imagine sleeping on a bed plastered with bloody handprints or the print pattern from the Overlook Hotel. Forget the sweet dreams. Bring on the nightmares.

The Monster Under the Bed:

And speaking of nightmares, bedtime for horror addicts just isn't what it should be without your own personal monster under—or over—the bed. The bogeyman lurks in the shadows in many different countries using a variety of names, you'll find the bedtime frightener in everything from Mayan tales to Egyptian folklore. If you consider the bogeyman passé, and want something more ethnic, how about the Spanish El Ogro, the Afghani Newanay Mama, or the Singapore Ah Bu Neh Neh. There are actually dozens of international variants of the monster under the bed (or in the closet). But he's not the only one posing a threat to potential sleepers. While he creeps in from below, evil fey and demons threaten those who slumber from above. Folklore includes differing tales of hag-riders or devil-riders who embark upon an unwary sleeper in the night. If you are lucky enough, they'll only torment you. The not so lucky will meet their end via suffocation.

Fright Lights:

My nine year old goes to sleep with the pleasing glow of an artificial moon and stars on his ceiling and walls, but I'm inclined to something more extreme. You can find the right night light out there to jar you into sleep if you look hard enough. My quest for a more frightful light carried me to the Poison Skull, Plasma bulb, and UFO night lights at Weburbanist.com. If that isn't scary enough for you, I also came across an alien face-hugger nightlight on Etsy.com. There's nothing like instilling the horror of being eaten from the inside out to drive you screaming into dreamland.

I realize these suggestions may be the cause of insomnia in those of more mundane and delicate temperament, but they are great ways to make bedtime better for true horrorphiles. They make fitting gifts, too, for the horror fans on your list.

What a special way to say goodnight. Visions of serial killers dancing in your head, anyone?

Gothic Tea Society

by Kristin Battestella

Kbatz here taking a midnight brunch this evening and spending a few moments with Wednesday Black, mistress and founder of The Gothic Tea Society website.

Kbatz: The Gothic Tea Society Page describes the Society's focus as attention toward "all those Macabre, Arcane, Creepy, and Dark things we can't get enough of" in addition to the promotion of the Gothic Culture and arts. How did the creation of the blog come about? Why did you feel the need for such a site back in 2009?

Wednesday: I created the blog as a vehicle to explore, discuss, and visualize those things that I define as Gothic. While there is a general conception of what is Gothic in our shared cultures, there are also many subtle and not so subtle differences that just add to the complex beauty mixed with macabre that to me, defines Gothic.

My own concept of 'Goth' has a pretty wide-angled lens, so I knew that there would be others who might appreciate my eclectic tastes. I was right, there are lots of people with a similar view. I try to include all leanings of Gothic, from the most basic old school to the Cyber-goth crowd. I really think there is room for everyone.

One thing I focus on are dark and alternative artists. There are some really talented gothic-leaning artists out there and I have had a great time over the last few years being introduced to them, usually by the people who read The Gothic Tea Society Blog and Facebook page. This year, I have started a series of interviews with artists whose work I have found incredible. They are all so creative and talented, but they all have a different eye, and they all have interesting stories. I also use The Gothic Tea Society to promote artists, Gothic shops (online as well as brick and mortar), and events worldwide. All readers are encouraged to share their own wares or favorites. Of course, I always appreciate efforts to spread the word about The Gothic Tea Society Facebook page and blog. Anyone who follows The Gothic Tea Society Facebook page knows that I also welcome 'shameless self promotion.'

Khatz: The Facebook companion page for The Gothic Tea Society has over 20,000 likes. Did you ever think there was such a huge online community in need of refined Goth media?

Wednesday: Yes, I did. The great thing about The Gothic Tea Society is that there is something for everyone. As a result there are many readers who have a sense of 'gothic appreciation' but would not consider themselves to be Goth. I have had people write to say that they are 'Goth-curious' or that they enjoy things with a gothic feel, but due to a variety of reasons they aren't comfortable openly expressing it in their daily dress and decor.

Khatz: Once considered the nonconformists of the club, Goth stylings have become much more mainstream and wow, I want to say popular. Do you think there are still misconceptions about the Goth and underground communities today?

Wednesday: Sure there are. Most commonly that anyone 'Goth' has something to do with Satan or some sort of Anti-Religion agenda. That if someone finds beauty in 'darkness' it is because they are depressed and unhappy. In our culture (western) wearing black is for funerals and mourning so if you wear black all the time it is thought you crave sadness and despair.

Speaking for myself, I do adore death culture and by that I mean the beautiful art, history and ritual associated with it.

I am an avid cemetery lover and photographer. I also love skulls, skeletons, Halloween, and bats too! I find quite a bit of beauty in things macabre. But all that said, I do not enjoy slasher and bloody horror or violence. That surprises some people, but to me one is natural and the other quite unnatural and unnecessary.

Kbatz: How do you handle some of the hateful spammers and normals who erroneously think that any and all Goths, folks who dress in black, Halloween enthusiasts, Wicca practitioners, Satanists, Zombie survivalists, punk, emo, etc. groups are one in the same evil and scary people?

Wednesday: Actually, to date, I have rarely encountered that sort of internet troll harassment. The way I see it is, if my blog or page offends you in any way, then click off of it! You need not expose yourself to something that upsets or offends you. We all have that free will.

I am careful to keep clear of anything political and I will delete any post that attempts to get political. I will also not allow rants or porn posts on The Gothic Tea Society. There are lots of pages and places for those things, GTS is not one of them.

Anyone who groups all the people that you mentioned under one label does so out of their own ignorance. I personally don't have time to debate with the uninformed.

Kbatz: The GTS offers news, interviews, and photos both Victorian and sophisticated and modern or punkish in humor.

How do you define Goth for yourself and the Society? Are the sub divisions, Goth specializations, and new labels good or bad do you suppose?

Wednesday: As I mentioned, I try to include photos, stories, and links that someone with very eclectic Gothic tastes might enjoy. I am sure not everything is for everyone, but I try for a good mix and I think I do okay.

I have a pretty encompassing Gothic scope. In my view, something is 'Goth' if it has a certain, sometimes undefined dark beauty, or melancholy aura about it. It is more of a feeling of macabre esthetic that defines it for me. I feel it as much as I see it.

I think the various sub divisions are great. Each one exists because someone said "Yes, this feels like me, but I also want to add this twist." They add it and a new look, music or piece of art is created.

Khatz: You also helm several more creepy sites and pages including The Daily Witch, November Obscura, and Wednesday's Attic. How do you manage such an online active lifestyle? Do you have a specific schedule or is it certain arcane material per page?

Wednesday: The Daily Witch is a fun eclectic witchery page on Facebook, created for the sole purpose of sharing my favorite witchy finds from around the net. I try to post at least one thing daily, but sometimes it doesn't work out that way.

November Obscura is a company that my husband and I founded together as an outlet for our photography and travel projects. It has a blog and a Facebook page as well. We have a plethora of blog posts upcoming on that one. Currently there are all sorts of topics in the blog, including lots of cemeteries!

Wednesday's Attic is my personal blog. There I post about things that I find interesting. I find many odd things of interest so I include things like that. It is somewhat macabre and strange because, well, it is my blog.

Schedule! That is a word that follows me around quite a bit because I spend at least five days a week on a tight one! I work full-time with a very long commute. I use the commute to plan blog posts, interviews and projects. Okay, sometimes I talk on the phone too, but hands free of course!

I use a little time before and after work each day to check in with my funny creative and interesting friends on Facebook on my own page, then share, and post on The Gothic Tea Society's Facebook. If I have a blog to post, such as an interview, I usually do that after work on a weeknight. I also have a few incredibly clever friends that I have met through The Gothic Tea Society that contribute to the blog. I have taken notice of them for their original style, creativity, and keen wit and I invite them to become contributors to the blog. They are marvelous! I am open to guest bloggers as well. It can be time consuming, but it is a labor of love.

Kbatz: Who are some of your inspirations or favorites of the aforementioned macabre or creepy in literature or television and film? What music are you listening to right now?
Wednesday: I was always a huge Anne Rice reader. My favorite books are ones about death rituals, art, and cultural mores. History, religion, and folklore.
Most of my TV watching consisted of documentaries or historical biographies, that was until I became hooked on *Six Feet Under* and then *Dexter*. (I am sensing a theme!)

I confess to being a rather Burtonesque style Goth. I give Mr. Burton quite a bit of credit for bringing black and purple out into the light of day, and making it 'cool' to love the arcane and creepy! His movies and characters have allowed a great many people to embrace the creepy they didn't even know they had in them.

As for music, unlike most who find their way to Goth through music, I found my way through art and other visual media. My preferred music is found between 1920 and 1950. I particularly love violin, cello and piano. I am not listening to anything now, except my cat who is complaining to me.

Kbatz: What social advice or styling tips would you give to the budding Goth enthusiast? How is one to stay true to themselves and not be a poser in today's era of trends, changes, and wannabes?

Wednesday: Find what you like, what feels good for you and go from there. I don't think there are hard defining lines on things like 'what is gothic' anymore so terms like poser and wannabe are obsolete. The only boundaries that exist are the ones you put up or allow. It's okay to be eclectic.

Kbatz: What's your favorite part of administering The Gothic Tea Society?

Wednesday: The fabulously interesting readers! I have met so many fascinating people.

Kbatz: Thanks Wednesday for taking the time to speak to me for HorrorAddicts.net.

Wednesday: My pleasure. Thank you for your interest in The Gothic Tea Society! Infect others!

To get in on the Goth action yourself, visit The Gothic Tea Society at:

gothicteasociety.blogspot.com

inspiring horror

nightshade on inspiration

What inspires you to live a horror lifestyle?

In this chapter, we have six articles where people talk about what inspired them to love horror. For most people, a love of horror started at an early age. You might have caught the bug while trick or treating as a kid and seeing all the neat costumes, and then thinking how much fun it would be to scare other people. Maybe you heard someone read a ghost story and it gave you a thrill, or maybe it was finding something scary on TV to watch, knowing if your parents were around they wouldn't let you. You watched it anyway, but you kept covering your eyes because you didn't think you could handle it.

For me, it was going to a horror movie and watching people scream in terror at something on the big screen that couldn't really hurt them. I love to hear people scream and I'm not sure why people like to go to non-scary movies. I feel sorry for those people watching dramas in the theatre and I try to help them see the error of their ways. I love to go into a sad movie and every time a new character comes on screen, I stand up, point to the screen and yell: "Oh my gawd! A werewolf!" My hope is that I'm livening up what looks like a dull movie. True, some don't appreciate it, and I get thrown out, but that just makes me dress in costume for the next flick! I love a reason to dress up.

☠

The Kings of Horror

by Dean Farnell

Vincent Price got it right,
With his mastered eerie voice.
Hammer Horror I bow to you.
You made the perfect choice.

The Werewolf he was played by Lou,
And particularly hairy.
When that moon was rising,
Things got a little scary.

Michael Myers and Jason,
Who lurked behind the mask,
Bumped off teenage scumbags.
What a joyous task.

Count Dracula depicted
By Bela, Christopher,
Perfect vampire legends.
Can't choose which I prefer.

Peter Cushing's steely stare,
His face it never laughed,
The coolest of the masters,
An unrivaled horror craft.

Boris Karloff's monsters face,
Made by Frankenstein.
No one better came along,
With a face made so divine.

The Munsters and The Addams,
The ideal family.
I found them all delightful,
The perfect guests for tea.

Finally your acting skills,
I'm not trying to be funny.
It seemed a wasted talent,
For those that played the Mummy.

vincent and me

by Garth von Buchholz

I wanted to meet Vincent Price. In the late '80s, Vincent was in his seventies, but still famous to my generation for his kitschy horror cameos in music, movies, and TV. His voice was heard in Alice Cooper's music, he narrated the early Tim Burton animated film *Vincent*, and he even appeared on *Scooby-Doo* cartoons, *Sesame Street*, and TV commercials, such as the one for a bug zapper device. His last major film role was the Inventor in *Edward Scissorhands*. Vincent was everywhere, and all his tongue-in-cheek, campy horror, carried off with a metaphoric wink of the eye and the chilling laugh, made him into an iconic pop culture personality.

To most people, Vincent was no longer scary. He didn't start his career trying to be scary. In the '40s, he was a handsome leading man in gothic romance potboilers such as *Laura* (1944) and *Dragonwyck* (1946). By the '50s he was doing television roles and appearances, then began his descent into the maelstrom of pop horror by starring in such classics as *The Fly* (1958), *Return of the Fly* (1959), and, of course, the Edgar Allan Poe adaptations by Roger Corman (1960-64). He brought his old world Hollywood gravitas to these sensational flicks, but even though he was creating a niche for himself, he was also losing credibility as a serious actor. Hollywood proper wouldn't come calling until years later when Tim Burton wanted him.

By the '60s, Vincent was already becoming parodied, and in fact, he helped parody himself to the younger generation in *Dr. Goldfoot and the Bikini Machine* (1965) and in his famous role as Egghead in the old *Batman* TV series (1966-67). By the '70s, Vincent was everywhere, a true journeyman actor. He appeared in the brilliant monologue series *An Evening of Edgar Allan Poe* (1972), the black comedy *Theater of Blood* (1973), and even on episodes of *The Brady Bunch* (1972) and *The Love Boat* (1978). Clearly, Vincent liked to work, had no pretensions about himself as an actor, and had a very dry sense of humor. He simply wanted to pay the bills and earn enough money to support his two true loves: his wife, Australian actress Coral Browne, and his extensive art collection.

As a fan of Poe, I had tremendous respect for the work he did on *An Evening of Edgar Allan Poe*, which you can still see in clips on YouTube. When I heard that he would be appearing in my city to perform poetry by Edgar Allan Poe on stage, accompanied by live music, I decided I had to meet him. As a young writer and journalist, it wasn't difficult for me to arrange complimentary tickets and a backstage pass to meet him before the show.

On the night of the show, I was ushered backstage to his dressing room. He was sitting at his dressing room table applying stage makeup under the bright globe lights above the mirror. When he caught sight of me, he turned with a broad smile and stood up, like a gentleman, to shake my hand.

"Hello, I'm Vincent Price," he said, as if an introduction was necessary. His skin pallor was very pale because he had not completed his makeup yet, but his eyes were remarkably clear, and he was a tall, elegant man who stood more than six feet in height. It was like meeting a crown prince or duke from Europe. He was the personification of noble grace and elegance. I felt like a thick-tongued commoner in his presence.

37

I gave him a copy of my own book of poetry as a gift and an introduction. How unembarrassed I was to do that shameless bit of self-promotion! I explained that I had been a fan of his for many years, and loved his work in the Poe stories. He said that he very much enjoyed doing them as Poe was a wonderful writer. He told me he was looking forward to his performance that evening, although it would require some effort because he had to modulate his voice so the orchestra would not drown him out during some key moments.

As I knew he was preparing to go on stage soon, I thanked him profusely and bid him farewell so that I wouldn't be in the awkward position of having the stage manager appear to shoo me away. His performance that evening was breathtaking, made even more voluptuous and dramatic because of the orchestra's choice of atmospheric works such as the spooky "Night on Bald Mountain". I can still recall him intoning the words from Poe's "Alone", "The Raven", and "The Conqueror Worm", the last of which made the greatest impression on me. Whenever I re-read "The Conqueror Worm", I can still hear Vincent's voice.

A few weeks later, the venerable Mr. Price sent me a postcard with a contemporary painting on the front and a few words on the back, thanking me for my book of poetry. This correspondence was an unexpected pleasure, a final goodbye from a famous acquaintance who had endeared himself to me not only for his talent, but for his gentility and generosity. Did he actually read the book or simply toss it on a pile in his library? I believe he did read it. There was an honesty and forthrightness in his reply.

Vincent Price died on October 25, 1993, after completing his final work—ironically, it was voiceover work for an animated movie called *The Princess and the Cobbler*. He never lived long enough to see how the World Wide Web would become a new medium to perpetuate his legacy as an actor, performer, entertainer, and pop culture persona.

No need to say goodbye. Your ghost is still with us, Vincent.

how hammer horror changed my life

by Sandra Harris

Growing up, I was always aware of Hammer Horror, the name given to the films made by the British production company founded in 1934 by businessman and comedian William Hinds. Ah yes, that lethal combination of businessman and comedian! You can't beat it. I knew that films bearing the name of Hammer—the ones I was familiar with from my childhood, anyway—were all shrouded in a supremely Gothic veil of mystery and suspense.

I knew the films told thrilling stories about vampires, Frankenstein's monster, and mummies from ancient Egyptian times. They also had stories about witches, yetis, and gorgons along with other weird and wonderful entities. I associated the films with rich colours—especially red, always red, the distinctive Hammer red—and majestic, crashing soundtracks that had the hairs standing up on the back of my neck long before the music reached its crescendo.

I associated them too, with beautiful young women with long lustrous locks and ample bosoms that always seemed to be spilling out over the tops of their tightly-waisted, low-cut gowns. An ex-boyfriend of mine confided in me once that when he was a lad, he *loved* watching Hammer films because you were nearly always guaranteed a flash of boobies or sometimes even the well-rounded posterior of a Hammer actress.

Certainly, films like *The Vampire Lovers* (1970) and *Lust for a Vampire* (1971), two of my personal favourites which feature scenes of lesbianism and full or partial nudity, would fit that bill. The Hammer girls, many of whom (Caroline Munro, Valerie Leon, Madeline Smith, etc.) went on to become fully-fledged sex symbols with deeply loyal followings, were for the most part top totty with cracking tits. You'll excuse my use of the vernacular. It's all in keeping, I assure you, with the fond affection in which these ladies are held, even to this day.

Mind you, the Hammer birds weren't just good at looking all fit and bosomy. They were also the best screamers in the business. Bloody hell, those broads could scream! I always loved the close-ups of a pretty female victim's face just before the vampire, or whatever monster it was, revealed itself. First, the welcoming smile, then the widening eyes as the busty young female realises that she might just possibly be in mortal danger, then the mouth opens wide and finally, we hear it. A blood-curdling, ear-splitting scream that could probably be heard several villages over in the realms of the mythical middle-Europe of bygone centuries Hammer recreated so beautifully in their films.

Ah, middle Europe as brought to us by Hammer Films! Sigh. It was a land of castles, carriages, beautiful women in cloaks, twisted, gnarly woods, and thorny bushes in eerie impenetrable forests. A land of tumbledown stone cottages and coach-men who refuse to drive you any further into the forest because the sun's just gone down.

You never knew what untold terrors might walk by night in the woods, just waiting for their chance to prey on unsuspecting travelers. I love it all. If I could live there, I would. Sadly, this magical land created for us by the Hammer scriptwriters doesn't exist outside of the films—and my head—but when you watch the films, you go there. That's how real it is. Let me fast-forward now, dear reader, to the Christmas of 2013. For a long time, I hadn't seen any Hammer movies. Life and other shit had gotten in the way, as it tends to do. Hammer Horror had sadly receded into the furthermost recesses of my mind in which I store "Brilliant Stuff That Made Me Happy Growing Up." Then BBC2 put on a brief season of Hammer Horror films late at night. For four nights over the course of Christmas week, I stayed up late and watched *Dracula* (1958), *The Curse of Frankenstein* (1957), *The Mummy* (1959), and *The Abominable Snowman* (1957).

I was glued to every single one of them. The house could have burned down around me while I was watching and I wouldn't have cared. I goggled at the richness of the colours. Again, red seemed to predominate, along with regal blues, purples, and dark greens. I listened avidly with racing pulse to the music that soared—literally soared—to magnificent and thunderous crescendos. I stared open-mouthed as Christopher Lee and Peter Cushing, Hammer's most famous and best-loved actors, slugged it out in Dracula's castle. Peter Cushing as Dr. Van Helsing, eventually emerges victorious. Because Dracula, sadly, must die at the end of each film in which he appears and always in a different manner. It's never for long, though, and Christopher Lee as the cloaked one does die so magnificently, it's worth the trauma just to watch him do it. I shivered deliciously as Peter Cushing stared up, wide-eyed and terrified, into the eyes of the Yeti high above the clouds in the Himalayas. I watched and listened, and something clicked into place in my brain. For me Hammer Horror had made a spectacular comeback, and this time, it wouldn't be going away anytime soon.

Things seemed to happen pretty quickly after that. When Christmas ended, I rushed out to my local DVD emporium and bought every Hammer film I could get my hands on, starting with the four I'd seen over the festive season. These four films were made during what has been referred to as the 'Golden Age' of Hammer Horror. Which lasted from the mid-fifties to the mid-seventies when they produced their most popular films. This was a time when directors like Terence Fisher—my favourite because he did the first *Dracula*—Michael Carreras, Roy Ward Baker, Peter Sasdy, and Freddie Francis coaxed stellar performances from an outstanding and predominantly British stable of actors and actresses. I watched and re-watched these films till I could recite them by heart. They never failed to thrill me.

Spurred on by the knowledge that Christopher Lee carried a copy of Bram Stoker's *Dracula* with him on the set of the films of the same name, I finally sat down and read the book myself for the first time from cover to cover. I bloody *loved* it! Though it was nowhere near as hard to read as I'd been led to believe, I was still inordinately proud of myself for having successfully gotten through it. I hurried to the Irish Writers' Museum up on Parnell Square here in Dublin and respectfully ogled first editions of *Dracula* and other works by the great man himself who was Irish like me. I then went to Marsh's Library, Ireland's oldest library, just up the road from Saint Patrick's Cathedral (and my house). There, I sat in the same chair in which Bram Stoker would have parked his famous butt when doing research on non-Dracula-related stuff prior to penning the work that made him a household name. My own butt, well aware of its comparative unworthiness, quivered in awe at the sheer buzz of it.

Excited beyond belief at having found a new purpose in life, I joined a handful of Hammer Horror Facebook groups and instantly made a bunch of new friends. These were lovely people who were all obsessed—in a good way—with the films made on the banks of the Thames in Bray Studios, Hammer's best-remembered base. I spent—and still spend—many happy hours chatting with them about the merits of one director over another and the importance of the distinctive musical scores in making the films as memorable as they were. They're all good people. I hope I'll remain friends with them for a long time to come. Their affection for and loyalty to the Hammer brand is unshakeable. Some of them are old enough to remember seeing films like *Dracula* (1958) in the cinema when they were first released. I can't even imagine how mind-blowing that must have been. Many of them have met iconic Hammer actors and actresses such as Christopher Lee, Peter Cushing, Ingrid Pitt, Caroline Munro, and Veronica Carlson in person. In person, lucky bastards!

One day I posted in one of these groups an account of how much I'd enjoyed watching one of my favourite Hammer films, *The Satanic Rites of Dracula* (1973). I'd included a few comments on what I considered to be the strong points of the film and how handsome and sexually dominant and smolderingly sexy Christopher Lee looked as he seduced and 'vampirised' a young abducted woman. You know, important stuff like that. Someone in the group complimented me on a 'great little mini-review' of the film. Or fillum, as we say here in Ireland. Film review? Me, review films? You can probably see where this is going.

Before long, an idea took root in my mind. I would indeed review films. I would review them on my first ever blog, which I would call SandraFirstRuleofFilmClubHarris. From the movie, *Fight Club*, right? You know, "The first rule of Fight Club is, you don't talk about Fight Club." Of course you do. I owned a boxset of 100 largely forgotten-about horror films that I'd thrown in a corner shortly after I'd bought it and...erm...largely forgotten about. I dusted it down and began to watch the films and review them one by one, sharing the results in the Facebook horror groups I joined. I also reviewed on my blog every Hammer film I owned and shared these reviews in the Hammer Horror Facebook groups.

I was delighted at the reception my reviews got. It turned out I had seriously underestimated the desire of people wanting to talk about films they either love or hate, but mostly love. Before long, I had followers. People who actually wanted to read my opinions on this film or that film, and not just Hammer movies, either. I included on my blog reviews of movies I discovered through my involvement in the online horror groups. Movies mostly from my favourite period, British and American horror films from the '70s and '80s. A whole new world of good horror films—and books—opened up to me in front of my eyes.

I'd been given a new lease of life. I was discovering a facet to my personality that had previously lain dormant. I was suddenly a film blogger and someone who could talk with authority on horror films. I was someone who could watch films and read books like Robert Bloch's *Psycho*, Stephen King's *The Shining*, and Shirley Jackson's *The Haunting of Hill House*. Previously I felt these would be too scary for me, and therefore, forbidden and closed off. I had the confidence to approach them now. I couldn't believe it. I was like a whole new person. My life was becoming virtually unrecognisable from what it had been less than a year ago.

I took to blogging like the proverbial duck to water. Within three months I'd been nominated for the "One Lovely Blog" award for my film blog. I decided to start a second blog for the filthy-dirty sex-poems I've been writing for years and which I perform in different venues around Dublin. I started a third blog to showcase my novel, *The Deviants*, which I write under the pen-name of Serena Harker. It's the story of the kinky-as-hell adulterous relationship between a married man and a much younger woman and I have high hopes for it. The most dramatic development, however, came about when I realised that I was hopelessly, irresistibly and irrevocably attracted to Christopher Lee's Dracula.

Christopher Lee, of course, is sex-on-legs no matter what role he's playing, but as Dracula? PHWOARRR! I wrote my very first piece of Dracula fan-fiction at a Creative Writing workshop I attended. I called it *Anna Meets Count Dracula* and I set it in Victorian London circa 1888, the Jack The Ripper era, a pretty optimum time for vampires. It's primarily about a beautiful young woman called Lady Anna Carfax (Carfax, geddit?!) who is seduced and carried off by Dracula to his secluded castle in the heart of the English countryside. Under Dracula's expert guidance, Anna experiences a sexual awakening so intense and powerful it changes her life forever. There are many other characters in the story too, each of whom has their own little quirks and idiosyncrasies, which I hope I exploit to the fullest!

As I write the stories, it's Christopher Lee's Dracula—the best screen Dracula ever in my humble opinion—whom I picture as my leading male character. He's charismatic, coldly handsome, sexually dominant, and dangerous as hell. Although the first ever *Anna Meets Count Dracula* story undeniably contained enough ham and cheese to fill a good-sized sandwich, it went down well, both at my Creative Writing workshop and on Facebook. That was all the encouragement I needed. Having gotten a positive reaction to my first story, I decided to write more instalments, serialise them on my film blog and share them around in all the Facebook horror groups, starting with the Hammer ones.

The stories are fun to write, scandalously and unashamedly sexy and, I hope, well-written. The response to this, my most ambitious writing project to date, has been fantastic. I have my little core group of die-hard fans, but all the time I have new people 'friending' me as well from the Facebook horror groups and telling me that they love the stories and they can't wait to read the next instalment. Their enthusiasm for the Anna stories both humbles and excites me. At the time of writing this article, I've written and posted thirty instalments and I'm well on my way to completing a full-length book. When I'm done with my *Anna Chronicles*, I'm planning on doing a sequel, again featuring Christopher Lee's Dracula as my handsome anti-hero.

My ultimate dream would be to turn these stories into an e-Book and for the great Sir Christopher Lee himself to read and approve of them. But even if he never sees them, I'll have the satisfaction of knowing that my little tribute to him is making its way out into the world anyway. The future's bright. The future's Hammer Horror. And I can't wait for it. Thanks, Hammer, for changing my life for the better. I love all of you guys forever. ☻

la LloRona scaRed and
inspiRed me

by Patricia Santos Marcantonio

As a kid in Pueblo, Colorado, I lived down the street from a cemetery, which to any horror fan is like living near Disneyland.

The cemetery was old. A six-foot tall stone and crumbing fence surrounded the place which we ignored during the day. But nighttime was another matter. Facing our street was a black iron gate in the cemetery wall and a lone light above that threw off a yellow illumination not only attracting bugs, but evil. Just inside the gate, was a gravestone with the name Frankenburg or something like that. To us, however, it became Frankenstein's resting place, or unresting place. We used to dare each other to touch the stone and live to tell the story. I tried once. My fingers grazed the cool marble. I swore I heard Frankenstein moan, or maybe it was Frankenburg.

Before the days of zombie videos, my friends and cousins tried to outdo one another in scaring the socks off each other in the evenings before our parents called us in for the night. And as Latinos, we specifically terrified each other with sightings of La Llorona.

We all knew the story of La Llorona, which had been told to us by our parents. As a result, the variations are many but this is the one my sister and I heard. The story starts with a beautiful, selfish woman who loved to party and keep company with men. One day, she drowned her children so she could run off with a man. God swept the babies to heaven, but his wrath fell upon the woman. Her once lovely face turned demonic from her wickedness. Her hair became white as mist and gnarled as angry snakes, and her eyes were blood red from incessant weeping for her lost children. She is doomed to forever walk the night in search of her children, crying out in a hideous squeaky voice, "Where are my babies? Where are my babies." La Llorona means the weeping woman.

Although not exactly a cozy bedtime story, the tale was meant to keep youngsters away from strangers. But to us, the weeping woman was just another monster from which to hide or run from. In fact, she ranked right up there with vampires and Frankenstein. (The zombie craze had not yet hit back then.)

In front of the cemetery, the cousins would yell, "It's the Llorona!" We would spin and swear we could see her, or at least imagine seeing her, dragging twisted feet and wearing a dirty ragged white gown. We'd scream out of the very real fear—for it is real fear when you are nine—that she would indeed grab us with claw covered hands and take us to hell or drown us, like she did her poor children. We'd scatter, then return to the spot under the cemetery light and wonder what other monster we could spot.

Those were the good times.

I owe a lot to La Llorona. She scared me then and in part inspired me to become a writer. Hers was just a darned good story. It also made me want more horror tales.

I stayed up reading *Tales from the Crypt* comics and H.P. Lovecraft books that I picked up in second-hand stores. Sure, I loved to read fairy tales and all those other good kids books, but give me a good scare every time.

I never missed Friday night horror movies on TV. One night, when my father worked a late shift, my sister, my mom, and I huddled together watching the original *Invasion of the Body Snatchers*. We trembled when an unformed alien body oozed out of one of those bizarre pods. We didn't want to close our eyes in sleep for fear there were pods underneath the bed, ready to replace us.

Ah, what memories.

As I grew up, my love of horror continued. Vampires were among my favorites. Not the cute Edward Cullen kind, but the bloodsuckers whose eyes were gorged with blood from their latest victims. To this day, I am a particular fan of Christopher Lee's version in the British Rank Films. Now that is one vampire you don't want to see outside your window.

My love of the horrific in books, graphic novels, television, and movies continues. Why? It is true, the more scared you are, the more you feel alive. But there is something else. Perhaps, it is because of a sad humanity behind the monsters and creatures. There's a tragic unfairness when a man grows hair and fangs through no fault of his own, when you happen to move into a house built over a cemetery, when the devil has its eye on you, or you're stuck in a spaceship with a malevolent alien. There is also bravery in how people face a Michael Myers, Jigsaw, anyone carrying a chainsaw, and a zombie licking its lips for your brain.

I do write children's books, dramas, and romance. But horror is well, special, all because of La Llorona. She inspired me, and her tale is part of my culture and childhood. I have written about the weeping woman in a short story, play, and now a novel. She taught me what it was like to be scared.

Sometimes, my husband and I walk our dogs at night. Up ahead under a street light, I still wonder if La Llorona lurks in the shadows, crying for her doomed babies, claws out, and ready to strike.

Touched by a Ghost

by Loren Rhoads

After I paid for the first Haunted Mansion Writers Retreat, I worried what I'd do if the mansion really was haunted. I wouldn't be able to drive to Mount Tamalpais for the long weekend, since I couldn't leave my family without a car. If I caught a ride with a stranger, I would be trapped at the mansion. What if things got really bad and I was afraid to sleep? I wouldn't be able to slink out to my car and sleep in it.

I also couldn't call my husband—assuming the isolated mansion got cell reception—to come and get me in the middle of the night. No way could I ask him to get our seven-year-old up, put her in the car seat, drive across the Golden Gate Bridge, and rescue me from the ghosts. If I went, I had to stick it out.

Probably, I told myself, if it got that bad, someone else would have the sense to want to leave. I could ride back to the ferry or a bus stop with them.

Of course, I was pretty sure that we wouldn't face an all-out *Poltergeist*-style freak out. As I packed for the weekend, my new worry became that I'd spent a couple hundred dollars to write for a weekend in a haunted mansion—and nothing would happen. The ghosts would ignore us, or they'd prowl around downstairs while we were all upstairs asleep. How disappointing would that be?

See, I have a healthy respect for ghosts. I've seen their shadows since I was a kid. Generally, they don't do anything more than make the hair on the back of my neck stand up. I feel cold and slightly jittery. Most of the ghosts I've seen were people I knew, or at least people I recognized. They weren't trying to scare me.

My body's reaction to them was scarier than anything they ever did.

Rain Graves, hostess of the Haunted Mansion Retreats, hadn't told us much about the ghosts that she'd encountered in the mansion. She wanted us to have our own experiences, to form our own opinions. So I went into the retreat blind, knowing no one other than her.

I met Scott and Eunice for the ride over to Mount Tam. Eunice had come up from Southern California; Scott would drive the two of us from San Francisco's Marina District across the Golden Gate. I was relieved to find them your typical very nice horror writers. They made me feel comfortable, like I wasn't making a terrible mistake going away with strangers to a haunted house for the weekend.

We arrived at the Haunted Mansion in the middle of Thursday afternoon. As we carried our bags into the mansion, Rain was standing on the grand staircase. She offered to give us a tour, so we could pick our rooms for the weekend. We hurried to move our luggage into the first-floor parlor and followed her up the stairs.

The second floor was a maze of interconnecting rooms that encircled the stairway. Almost everyone else had come with a friend with whom they planned to share a room. Since I was solo, I wavered between asking to share someone else's room or taking a room of my own. Would the ghosts be more or less likely to mess with me if I slept alone?

There were only eight of us there that first night, rattling around in a house that seemed able to sleep a hundred. Rain said we would all stay on the second floor, even though that was where she'd had the most intense of her ghostly encounters. Most of the second-floor rooms were pass-throughs: each dormitory-style room connecting to the next. I don't sleep well at the best of times, so I wasn't eager to choose a room where people might walk through in the night to use the bathroom. Since I wander a fair amount when I can't sleep, I also didn't want to wake anyone else.

Rain's tour paused outside a little blue room tucked between a suite—reserved for the one married couple among us—and dead space. I'm not sure what lay on the other side of the wall: maybe a linen closet? It wasn't another guest room, anyway.

The blue room felt very restful to me, very welcoming. It helped that it only had one door, which faced the bed, and a window that looked out on Mount Tam. The energy felt inviting. When I stepped inside and saw the artwork hanging above the vanity—a piece of white silk featuring a bright Chinese phoenix—I had to have that room. I wear a phoenix tattoo on my left arm. The room and I shared a kinship.

After midnight, My little room proved to be a great haven, especially after I set my suitcase in front of the large walk-in closet. Not that I thought anything was going to come through there—or that I felt the suitcase provided much of a barricade—but I've seen *Poltergeist* too many times. You never know with big empty spaces.

I settled into the double bed, feeling safe in a way I wouldn't have in a room with more doors. I closed my eyes, exhausted and slightly drunk from Rain's good Argentinean wine.

Sleep wouldn't come.

I thought I heard whispering voices, then a man speaking, but Yvonne and Weston had the suite that shared the minuscule balcony outside my spider-guarded window. I gladly put on my headphones to block the voices out.

As I lay there in the dark, trying to sleep, the light in my room kept changing. Smudges and smears of light flashed through the well of shadow that lay between the bed and the vanity. The sliver of light coming in around the door grew wider toward morning, as if the door was inching open, but it wasn't. Even so, I didn't turn my back toward the center of the room.

Finally, about 4:30 a.m., I told myself that I really needed to get some sleep. I rolled onto my stomach, clutched the pillow, and felt myself relax. Sleep was washing over me when someone touched my hair.

Someone touched my hair! Electricity thrilled through me. I knew I was still alone in the room, but opened my eyes anyway. The room remained silent and empty, holding its breath to see what I would do.

It occurred to me that a spider might have fallen from the ceiling on to me. However, the sensation of being touched hadn't felt like something practically weightless dancing across my head. My hair is just not that sensitive. Something the size of a hand compressed the hair on the right side of my head. Without a doubt, someone touched me.

"Hello," I whispered softly. "It will be dawn soon. I'd really like to get some sleep before then. Can we talk in the morning?"

I waited, but nothing more happened. Sleep was remarkably easy to find.

This is an excerpt from an essay I wrote for The Haunted Mansion Project: Year One, published by Damnation Books in 2013. I served as editor for The Haunted Mansion Project: Year Two, published by Damnation Books in 2014. Both

books collect fiction and poetry inspired by our retreats at the mansion. They also include reports of the hauntings we experienced and evidence reports by the GhostGirls.

For information about future Haunted Mansion Writers Retreats, go to:

http://hauntedmansionwriters.blogspot.com

on horror directing
by Willo Hausman

Being a director who is smitten with ghosts and monsters, I was immediately drawn to taking on the job of directing a theatrical version of Charles Dickens' haunting tale. When I think of *A Christmas Carol* I go immediately to the world the author so clearly created in this classic story. He wrote none of the schmaltzy, over-bright, happy-go-lucky stuff so often presented in this traditional holiday fare.

So, the first rule of thumb in taking on this endeavor, was that I would be allowed free rein to stick to the original story with all its strange and ominous intent. The elements that make this novel intriguing—and caused its incredible success—depict frightening ghosts (four of them to be precise), depressing poverty and illness, the permanence of death, and a central character that is an incredibly mean-spirited man, living his life in miserly bitterness. It is only at the very end that Scrooge is redeemed and if we have gone through this truly dark journey alongside him, experiencing all the nightmares he does, then we too will rejoice in his enlightenment, as well as our own.

I first pitched the idea of putting up *A Christmas Carol* to Steve Coleman, The Throckmorton Theater's fabulously gifted set designer. After realizing we were kindred artistic spirits and connected creatively in numerous ways, the notion of putting up this play burned that much brighter in my mind. I felt even more driven to direct this piece on that particular stage, surrounded by such appropriate ambiance. There is a very old-fashioned charm to this space in Mill Valley, California (it began as a cabaret in the

1920s) and it really rang true for the vision I had in mind for this production. This inspiration was fueled even further after reading a certain version of the script, written in England by Charles Ludlam. True to the original tale his version was shadowy, mysterious, witty and finally, upbeat.

As Scrooge enters the realm of his memories, confronts the truth of his present, and imagines a future without hope, we learn what truly matters; truth, kindness, and heart. What better way to impart lessons then with spooky apparitions, intense imagery, haunting realizations, rich dialogue, and in the end, utter spectacular joy? Dickens does it best with his original intent, just as the fairy tales of old were wont to do. With this production we planned to stick as close as possible to the real message within the author's words and use his inventive tactics to present them.

We ended up with a terrifically twisted and authentic set which ultimately went through 18 shifts during the show, carried out primarily by the performers themselves. A talented cast of twenty-five, ages 7-77, consisted of both professionals and amateurs. We used old-fashioned stage trickery like black-lights and human-made sounds to announce the arrival of Marley's ghost along with new-fangled elements such as nine fantastic projections depicting Scrooge's memories and ghostly travels, filmed by the masterful Mark Bowen. The mesmerizing live sound effects and incredible cinematic score composed by Steve Kirk, our composer, underlined the action and added to the shadowy mood. We also mixed in a few modern day splashes via our fantastic costume designer, Morganne Newson, who brought some steampunk hues to her slate of Victorian clothing. It was topped off with fantastically unique looks created by Maya Lopez and Leonie Meissner, our hair and make-up designers, who worked their magic on our diverse set of characters. Many of the actors played up to three roles each and needed to change looks fairly rapidly. After the initial opening night jitters, the play acquired a great rhythm and the audience (including Robin Williams) laughed and appeared in awe at all the right places. Happily, I even heard reports of some folk being rather frightened by the eerie specters and mesmerizing illuminations.

In the future I'm planning a grand scale version of *Frankenstein* and a play based on the intriguing life of my mother, actress Diane Varsi. In active development are two feature films: *Clare*, a murder mystery revolving around a clan of modern-day witches living in the midst of a bustling metropolis (screenplay by Maria Bernhard) and *Among the Wonderful* (based on a novel by Stacy Carlson); a vintage circus tale set at Barnum's NYC museum circa 1842 with a giantess and a taxidermist at the center of the mix. Also on the slate are a sitcom *The Vibe* (written by Jon Mosher), an Edward Gorey based film, a Buster Keaton bio-movie, and a documentary about mental illness. My next trilogy (*Grim*) is on the way to a first reading with a fantastic cast in the mix. Dark and true to the original fairy tales, three writers have adapted three of the tales (*The Juniper Tree, Rapunzel,* and *The Girl with No Hands*) for the stage.

viewing horror

nightshade on viewing

What is your favorite horror to view on screen?

If you ask me, the scariest things to watch on TV are reality shows. Do people actually like watching these? The only way I think you can make these shows fun is by adding a few monsters. For instance, a show like *The Biggest Loser* is kind of boring, I mean I really don't care if these people are overweight or not. But, it might be fun to add the vampires from *The Vampire Diaries* to *The Biggest Loser*. Think about it, the contestants in *The Biggest Loser* would be a lot more motivated to lose weight, if they thought a vampire would have an easier time catching them. The host would just have to say, "If you don't drop twenty pounds this week, the vampires get to eat you." Who needs a fitness trainer when you have vampires trying to feast on your blood?

I also think *Keeping Up with the Kardashians* would be a much better show if you added zombies from *The Walking Dead*. Everyone would be rooting for the zombies and hey, Kim has some big munching targets to make it easier on them. What about mixing a ghost/medium show like *The Dead Files* to *The Property Brothers*? "First, we have the shabby detached, twenty minutes out of town, with one grandma ghost. Second, we have the dream mansion, three minutes from work, filled with shadow people and a rather scary demon thing. Which house will you choose?" Maybe I need to become a television program director. I have some awesome ideas!

I know all of you love a good horror movie or TV show, so here are eight articles on horror viewing. Who reading this book hasn't stayed up watching horror movies all night or enjoyed a *Tales From the Crypt* marathon? There is lots of good horror on TV but you have to be willing to look for it. I love to watch TV in October, because you don't have to look as hard for something scary. Of course, now with the internet, you can make every night Halloween and have a horror marathon of your own.

top 10 horror flicks

by HorrorAddicts.net

As voted on by HorrorAddicts.net listeners

1. *The Exorcist*
2. *Suspiria*
3. *The Shining*
4. *Phantasm*
5. *Hellraiser*
6. *Bram Stoker's Dracula*
7. *Prince of Darkness*
8. *Inside*
9. *Night of the Living Dead* (original)
10. *Dracula* (Bela's)

top 10 horror tv series

by Kristin Battestella

1. *Buffy the Vampire Slayer*
2. *Dark Shadows*
3. *The Twilight Zone*
4. *Tales from the Darkside*
5. *The X-Files*
6. *Friday the 13th the Series*
7. *Tales from the Crypt*
8. *Night Gallery*
9. *Forever Knight*
10. *Elvira's Movie Macabre* (I'm cheating I don't care!)

Humorous Honorable Mentions:
The Addams Family
The Munsters

horror movie marathon

by J. Malcolm Stewart

Horror addicts, we need to have a serious chat.

It's about Halloween, you see. I've been hearing some of you are dressing up, going out and doing various social activities on October 31st. And as a resident horror movie buff and historian, it's my solemn duty to tell you... This behavior has to stop.

"Why?" you might be asking. "Why do I have to give up going out on October 31st?" Well, simply put, it's bad for you. Dressing up like some creature of the night, going around eating junk, scaring innocent villagers... You can do all that at home!

In fact, you need to go all-in with this "staying home on Halloween" thing. Lock the doors, take that sick day you've been saving, and bundle up to the TV or iPad and watch horror movies all day and night. Your stomach will thank you for it. And just think of the brain cells you'll save by not drinking the yearly Witches Brew!

Now, I can hear you saying, "Well, if I do skip leaving the house on Halloween, what films should I watch to pass the time?"

I'm glad you asked! I have your itinerary all planned out for you. Fifteen films you need to watch from 12:00 to 12:00, so you can make sure you use every iota of energy in the right way.

So, let's set your alarm and fire up that DVR...

12:00am-1:38am: *Sleepaway Camp,* **1983**: Felissa Rose's mind-bending, criss-cross killer starts our little cine-fest, mostly because this is a movie that demands you are fully present minded to follow the action. And if you're not paying attention, by the end, you will be. The eye opening last scene is just the thing you need to make sure you're wide awake and bushy tailed for the rest of the marathon. Better than a Five Hour Energy drink!

1:45am-3:20am: *Bug*, 2006: Listen, addicts, there's nothing better than watching a bunch of meth-heads freaking out on screen to get you through the early morning. Some might doubt the horror resume of this slow boiling thriller. But when Michael Shannon starts screaming "Machine! Machine!" there is no doubt you've taken the terror train to crazy land. Ashley Judd tears it up too. If you ever wanted to live the lyrics of Golden Earring's "Twilight Zone," now's your chance.

3:30am-5:00am: *A Nightmare on Elm Street*, 1984: Now, you might be feeling a little drowsy around the third watch of the night. Not to worry, once you cuddle up with Wes Craven's version of *NOES* and relive Robert Englund's merry havoc raising turn as Freddie, bed will be the last place you wanna end up. Besides, who wants to miss Johnny Depp biting the Big One in one of the most expensive death scenes in 80's horror film? Not me.

5:10am-6:35am *Wicked City*, 1987: The Land of the Rising Sun is served up for breakfast in this horror Anime classic. Giant spider women, big gooey monsters, and lots of swords will be better than OJ on this fine, fall morning. Skip the dubbed version and practice your Japanese with the original, director's cut. *Arigatou Gozaimasu*!

6:45am-8:20am: *Cronos*, 1993: Take a few minutes to slap together some peanut butter sandwiches for you and the kids and gather round for Guillermo del Toro's Mexican masterpiece. If seeing ancient clockwork blood-letting bugs doesn't make those PBJs taste just right, nothing will. Besides, everything goes better with milk, even crazed, grandfatherly vampires. *Salud*!

8:30am-9:57am: *Black Sunday "La Maschera Del Demonio"*, **1960:** If you know me (and if you don't, I'm inviting myself over), then the fact that you need your regular dose of director Mario Bava is not a surprise. The one that started it all for Italian Horror is still one of the most visually stunning films in the genre. Barbara Steele in the morning ain't bad neither, though her dubbed voice is a bit distracting. Look for all the scenes that have been swiped by Tim Burton, Rob Zombie, and others.

10:00am-11:10am: *The Wolf Man*, **1941:** You also really need some classic Universal Horror in your life today. And Lon Chaney, Jr.'s monster claim to fame is on this particular list. I hear some of you growling, "What about Whale's Frankenstein or Browning's Dracula? Why do we have to watch the chubby Chaney?" Well, mostly because of the supporting actors to LCJ, like Bela Lugosi, Claude Rains, and Olga Ouspenskaya. I think Universal knew Chaney Jr. was in over his head, so this film stands out for the all-time greats who kept the ship afloat.

11:20am-12:55pm: *Dead Alive*, **1992:** Just in time for lunch is Peter Jackson's slapstick gore-fest, straight from the Land Down Under. You'll be ready for some surf and turf after watching latex guts and strawberry jam, fly, splatter, and gush across your screen by the ton. Plus, if you can make it through the scene with the kung-fu fighting priest without shooting Coke through your nose, you're a better person than I am. (I mean the drink now!)

1:00pm-5:15pm: *The Evil Dead Trilogy:* Speaking of Peter Jackson, do you have those fantasy friends who watch the whole LOTR Saga periodically just so they can boast that they sat through nine hours of bad hair extensions and over-acted Elvish gibberish? Well, now's the chance to put them in their place by taking on the whole Sam Raimi epic in all its undead glory. What's better than four hours and fifteen minutes of Bruce Campbell's Ash? That's right...Almost nothing. Except possibly more horror movies.

5:25pm-7:15pm *Re-Animator,* **1985:** Let the sun go down on you watching Jeffery Combs bringing H.P. Lovecraft's favorite doctor to gruesome life. Hold out for the uncut extended edition which will bring you almost twenty more minutes of mayhem than the standard theatrical edition of the film. Hey, if you're gonna watch Herbert West get mauled by a twice dead cat, you may as well get your money's worth. H.P. would insist on it, along with another hit of the Green Fairy.

7:25pm-9:05pm: *The Serpent and the Rainbow,* **1988:** Dinner is the time of day to sit around the table and do some family bonding. And if you're watching Wes Cravens' voodoo classic, eat some glass as well. This 80's magical zombie romp starts low-key and then gets kooky. Where else can you go to see Paul Warfield throw his head at Bill Pullman? You'll give up sewing and Red Stripe Beer after this one.

9:10pm-10:34: *Night of the Living Dead,* **1968:** What more perfect film to watch on a night when everyone knocks at your door? You'll have reason not to answer as George Romero's touchstone masterpiece unfolds. Every zombie apocalypse story ever told follows the footsteps of Romero's ghouls and his black and white dismemberment scenes are still note-perfect even forty-five years later. Pass the popcorn twice!

10:35pm-12:05am: *Halloween,* **1978:** Of course, we are saving the best for last. Turn off the lights, warm up the hot cocoa and let Jamie Lee, Donald Plesance, and Tony Mornan take you away. What the original lacks in gore and grime, it makes up with tension and atmosphere. And the John Carpenter written and performed score is still one of the great pieces of horror music ever put to film. The icing on the cake as far as we're concerned.

What? "You wants some more?" Well, lucky for you addicts, stuff like this gets served up all the time at HorrorAddicts.net. And if you specifically need more movie madness, check out my book *Look Back In Horror: A Personal History of Horror Film* available on Amazon in paperback and eBook right now! And remember, this October 31st, in the immortal words of horror host, Bob Wilkins, "Keep America Strong...Watch Horror Film!"

bodyCounters.com

by Kristin Battestella

Kbatz is tallying the dead tonight with the gals from Bodycounters.com, Stacey and Dana!

Kbatz: First and foremost, how did the Body Counters come about in 2006?

Bodycounters: We were trying to get over some bad breakups and looking for ways to distract ourselves. We spent a lot of time drinking beer and watching movies together and since we didn't want to see any romances or love stories, we gravitated toward movies where a lot of people die. It was cathartic and helped heal our broken hearts, filling us with a love for counting bodies.

Kbatz: When did you envision that this could be such a wild website with your own merchandise and appearances at shows like Monster Mania?

Bodycounters: At first we just kept the list on a piece of paper, but as it started to grow longer than one page, we realized we needed to share this information with the rest of the world. Dana had a little experience with web design, so we bought the domain bodycounters.com and put the list up there for everyone to see. It was a few years before we added merchandise and started going to conventions like Monster Mania.

Kbatz: How did the rules come about?

Bodycounters: The rules developed over time. At first, we didn't have a rule about every body counting and only counted the humans, but the more movies we watched the more discussions we had about what should count and what shouldn't.

Kbatz: You encourage fans to 'harass' and contest your tabulations. Do people really complain, argue, and give you a tough time? Or are they all in the fun with the rules and counting?

Bodycounters: Some people do complain and argue, but we encourage that because we welcome the feedback. Sometimes a fan will come up with a question we hadn't thought of before or find a loophole in a rule that makes us go back and redo a count. Most people are very much in the spirit of it and all about the fun and try to stick to the rules. We love all our fans, even the ones that harass us!

Kbatz: You have a certain amount of snark on your website but your counts and statistics are very detailed and organized in searchable tables with voting options. Are the wit and methodical just part of your personalities or does the subject matter simply require the right amount of humor and precision?

Bodycounters: It's probably a little of both. That is definitely our personalities shining through in the comments and "awards" we give out to certain movies, and keep in mind this was just on a piece of paper in the beginning and just our own inside jokes. When you've watched over 1,500 movies with this level of attention to detail, you also start to notice how little things like lighting and music can make a big difference. And while we do like to have our fun and keep rule #10 enforced (Sobriety is expressly forbidden), we are also very serious about accuracy and making sure our counts stay true to all the other nine rules.

Kbatz: Viewers would presume that you are counting deaths in horror movies or looking for a lot of blood and bodies, but you review all genres of films with as little as no deaths or one or two bodies as well as tally apocalyptic deaths. How do you decide what movies to watch? What kind of body count do you prefer most?

Bodycounters: We try to let the fans decide what movies we watch for the most part. The to-do list on our page has voting buttons so we know what bodycounts everyone wants to see next. We also get a lot of suggestions at Monster Mania every year.

Our favorite kind of bodycount is one that has all of these things: a romance we can't handle, a renegade cop who plays by his own rules, a crazy/drunk old man who warns everyone but no one listens to him, a gratuitous shower scene, and of course it needs to have at least one body!

Kbatz: How does the Samuel Jackson motherfucker counting fall under the body counting rules?

Bodycounters: When *Snakes on a Plane* was getting all kinds of hype on the internet before its release, we loved how the fake trailers people made on the internet actually changed the future of the movie. Someone made a trailer where Sam Jackson said "I'm sick of these motherfucking snakes on this motherfucking plane" and the response from the internet was unbelievable. The movie producers pulled Sam Jackson back in to re-shoot that scene because it wasn't really from the movie but they knew everyone would be disappointed if their favorite line from the FAKE trailer wasn't in the real movie. This movie was our 100th bodycount (which seemed like a huge milestone at the time, now look at us), and we had a big party to celebrate. We thought it would be fun to also count the motherfuckers from Samuel L.

Jackson in addition to counting the bodies, and another statistic was born.

Khatz: You've done body counts for 1,500 films. Do you ever get tired of tallying the dead people, pets, and planets? Can Bodycounters.com go on indefinitely?

Bodycounters: No, we will never get tired of it! It has completely changed the way we watch movies. There is a steady stream of new movies getting made all the time, and we feel like we haven't even put a dent in the total film universe even though we have counted more than 1,500 movies. If we ever do find that we run out of movies to count maybe we'll consider TV shows…

Find out more about Bodycounters at:
<u>Bodycounters.com</u>

MoRE To offER Than blood and boobs

by James Newman

Seven first-class fright films to show the uninitiated.

For decades, the modern horror film has held a reputation of existing solely for the glorification of violence. Some of that is justified—the number of bad movies released in any given year certainly outnumbers the quality films that will stand the test of time. Horror fans shoulder much of the blame for the stigma attached to the genre. Many of us name among our heroes masked psychos who slash their way through bland, two-dimensional characters in sequel after sequel, and killers who can only be killed themselves by diminishing box-office returns. But there's so much more to the genre than death and dismemberment.

It's no wonder the "normal people" don't understand our love for scary movies, when gore and cheap jump-scares are the first things most of them think of when they hear the word HORROR. Cinema fans only need to dig a little deeper to find films within the genre that are not only genuinely scary, but artfully made and instilled with thought-provoking subtext.

Trying to convert a non-horror fan? Give these titles a shot.

TRICK R' TREAT (2007)

Trick r' Treat is a love letter to Halloween. You can almost smell the crisp autumn leaves, the mouth-watering aroma of caramel apples and pumpkin spice. The film's non-linear narrative is constructed from several different Halloween-related stories, but the tales in this anthology weave in and out of one another in a format similar to *Pulp Fiction*. See *Trick r' Treat*, and remember what it felt like to sit around a campfire with your buddies, telling ghost stories and urban legends, scaring yourselves silly. Who didn't love that?

LET THE RIGHT ONE IN (2008)

A poignant look at friendship as much as it is a horror film, *Let the Right One In (Lat Den Ratte Komma In)* is a Swedish vampire movie that's not afraid to do something different with a classic monster. A bullied teenager befriends a young lady (or is she?) who survives by drinking blood, but can even the strongest of friendships truly last forever? *Let the Right One In* is nothing less than a somber work of art, and is easily one of the best genre films of the last twenty years. 2010 saw an American remake called *Let Me In* (starring Chloe Grace Moretz from *Kick-Ass* and 2013's recent *Carrie* rehash), and that version is worth a watch too.

THE EXORCIST III: LEGION (1990)

A box-office flop due to audience expectations brought on by its predecessor (the wretched *Exorcist 2: Heretic*), this third installment in the *Exorcist* series is the true sequel to the classic original film, as it is based on writer/director William Peter Blatty's novel *Legion*. *The Exorcist III* follows Detective William Kinderman as he investigates a series of sacrilegious murders in Georgetown. Murders that appear to be committed by a killer who died in the electric chair. There's a disturbing link to a certain young lady, too—a troubled twelve-year-old who once sprayed profanities and pea soup on two priests. Despite an ending that feels completely out-of-place (forced upon Blatty by the studio), *The Exorcist III: Legion* is as terrifying as William Friedkin's original *Exorcist*. Especially that one scene. You'll know which one when you see it.

DEATHDREAM (1972)

A tragic look at how young men and women who are sent off to war often return as ghosts of their former selves, *Deathdream* (a.k.a. *Dead of Night*) is the story of Andy, a young man who is killed in Vietnam. But then his family is elated when he comes knocking at their door one night, seemingly safe and sound. Problem is, Andy now needs blood to stay alive. Eventually, his loved ones start to wonder if it would be best if he had never come home at all. A modern take on W.W. Jacobs' classic short story "The Monkey's Paw", *Deathdream* is an underrated gem from Bob Clark, who also made *Black Christmas*, *Porky's*, and *A Christmas Story*.

THE LOVED ONES (2009)

Lola asks Brent to take her to the prom. He politely turns her down. He'll regret it. This Australian horror film is a nerve-wracking descent into terror that some have called "*The Texas Chainsaw Massacre* meets *Pretty In Pink*" . . . and that's not too far off. While this one certainly has its share of gruesome moments, it's all about the psychological suspense when all is said and done. Robin McLeavy (TV's *Hell On Wheels*) turns in a devious performance that ranks among horror's all-time greatest villains, a rarity in a genre that usually restricts women to the role of helpless victims. "Hell hath no fury like a woman scorned", indeed.

IN THE MOUTH OF MADNESS (1994)

Once upon a time, John Carpenter was a master of horror, as evidenced by genre classics like *Halloween* (1978), *The Fog* (1980), and *The Thing* (1982). Sadly, *In the Mouth of Madness* is probably his last really good film. This one's about Sutter Kane, a best-selling horror author whose work has driven his worldwide fan base to acts of murder and madness. When Kane goes missing, an insurance investigator—played by genre fave Sam Neil (*Jurassic Park*, *Event Horizon*, *Omen III: The Final Conflict*)—is hired by the writer's publisher to find him. Before long, the hunter becomes the hunted, the lines between fiction and reality blur, and it's the end of the world as we know it.

SHUTTER (2004)

Make sure your uninitiated pal is okay with subtitles first. This wonderfully eerie film from Thailand takes the "long-haired ghost girl" trope so prevalent in Asian horror films like *Ringu*, *Ju-On*, et al, and makes it scary again. After a young man kills a woman in a hit-and-run accident on a deserted country road (or does he?), he's haunted by her ghostly visage at every turn. *Shutter* is worth seeing just for the last ten minutes, which feature one of the creepiest get-under-your-skin images in the history of modern cinema.

lady horror films
by Kristin Battestella

In the mood for some scary chick flicks? Here's a sampling of new and old lady vamps, witches, ghosts, werewolves, killers, with slightly—heck who are we kidding—outright feminine spins!

The Awakening I'm glad this 2011 ghost tale utilizes plenty of post-war traumas along with fun spiritualism and early ghost hunting gadgets, and a great, spooky English house turned boarding school which keeps the paranormal pace going, too. Although some of the said supernatural equipment and unnecessary character clichés are a touch too modern, the fractured Dominic West, perfectly nuanced Imelda Staunton, needs no one Rebecca Hall, and innocent Isaac Hampstead Wright keep the audience interested even when the back story gets confusing toward the finale. Are these ghosts, personal demons, and memories, or something more? There may not be enough scares here for a hardcore horror fan and wise viewers may see through the bump in the night clichés and saucy innuendo thanks to similar ghost films. However, this mood and atmosphere does what it sets out to do and fits the pain, loneliness, and isolation perfectly. Those period designs, cars, clothing, creepy dollhouses, and even the way they hold their cigarettes, keep the dramatic before scary scenes classy. Despite some brief nudity and a few twists, there are no contemporary cheap thrills here, and the mystery is intriguing enough to keep the viewer invested for the full 100 minutes.

Burn Witch Burn A creepy, blank screen opening narration sends this 1962 British thriller a-simmering beneath the campus innocence, great cars, ivy covered cottages, and seemingly fine period drama—but that's before they find the sudden spider souvenirs hidden in the bedroom drawer! Not so nice and magical wife Janet Blair has all sorts of *Craft* curios amid the great set dressings, cigarettes, period style, and black cats. It's a lighter take than most witchy pictures, but the secret practices are no less creepy thanks to sinister suspense music and scary discoveries. The well-framed, black and white prospective photography, mirror uses, and shadow schemes parallel the fractured, marital debates, too. Peter Wyngarde is a disbeliever relying on logic, education, and intelligence versus the implausibility of positive charms and evil hexes. Thunder, wind, eerie tape recordings, even the old-fashioned abrupt ringing of a telephone puts one on edge here, and the pace comes to a pinnacle to finish this excellent, deadly thriller.

Byzantium Gemma Arterton and Saiorse Ronan anchor this 2013 vampire spin from director Neil Jordan. The cinematography is intriguing, and a golden, antique patina contrasts the bitter daylight, nightclubs, boarded windows, and harsh concrete. Ironic uses of Etta James standards and melancholy piano music add to the slight sense of abstract. The contemporary still has a feeling of the past in old décor, fedoras, and aged computers. Nostalgic paper, pens, and handwriting or scandalous red lights and saucy lingerie establish the ladies' personalities better than narration, which takes too long for viewers who didn't know this movie would be about vampires. Fortunately, Arterton is sexy yet deadly and nude yet refined—she's a killer in every sense of the word—but bizarrely maternal, loving, and considerate. Although Ronan's depressing, woe-is-me burdens are a bit much, her somber, hypnotic blue eyes are classy and bittersweet. Her flashbacks provide interesting snippets of period piece macabre; the past wasn't glamorous but dirty, grimy, and violent. These ladies dab the blood from their lips, quietly wait for the invitation to enter, get tempted by the sight of blood and injury, and take the lives of the ill or elderly who watch Hammer movies! This isn't scary, and the assorted accents and Brit-ness may bother some. However, this isn't a sparkly teeny bopper love triangle either. The viewer doesn't always know what happens next in the intense finish, and this tale makes for a surprising, worthy piece of vampire storytelling.

Daughters of Darkness This 1971 Elizabeth Bathory suave and swanky Euro bend—starring John Karlen and Delphine Seyrig—gets right to the saucy, up close, wet, near soft core action and full frontal nudity. Aristocratic family secrets, deceptions, kinky newlyweds, and suggested lesbian jealousies add to the traditional vampire staples—from unexplained perpetual youth, lookalike ancestors, and a reflectionless countess with a beautiful, mysteriously bound ward to straight razor cuts on the neck, fear of running water, and no trace of blood at the scene of the crime. Toss in meddling, aged bellhops, astute old cops, the local morbid curiosity, and a bevy of babes—namely Danielle Oulette and Andrea Rau—and the murders, violence, and homoerotic twists are complete. The cars are seriously cool, too, as are the symbolic fashions, flashy frocks, and colorful velvet décor. The perfect Ostend Hotel and other European locales more than make up for the tacky but sassy and fitting music, and the nice mix of accents on the English dialogue adds more foreign flair to kinky descriptions of medieval torture—nipple pinchers, hot tongs, and all that. Red lighting and blue tinted photography add to the creepy jump scares and frights, but this isn't horror per se, rather something more voluptuous in mood. Remember, the key to beauty is "A very strict diet and lots of sleep."

Drag Me to Hell Sam and Ivan Raimi present this 2009 tale of curses and consequences starring Alison Lohman as the likeable and realistic Christine. She's trying to change her accent, forget her 'porker' past and family issues, and keeps doubting or compromising herself, yet she's also trying to pin her problems on someone else. Lohman carries the increasing paranoia nicely with honest pace and progression as her true colors come forth amid the good jump moments and the not so gruesome that it's overdone gore and grossness. Fortunately, most of the scares and suspense are well done what you don't see shadows and wind effects, and the Spanish spins and multi-language mythos add flavor along with Dileep Rao's unique take on the usually clichéd psychic. There are subtle _Evil Dead_ references, of course, but one can certainly laugh or be scared by this entertaining little flick, eyeball in the cake at the dinner party and all.

Ginger Snaps This quality Canadian horror drama is not for animal lovers and today, such teen sex, drug uses, school violence, juvenile morbidity, and obsessions with death would land sisters Katharine Isabelle and Emily Perkins in serious hot water. Director John Fawcett and co-writer Karen Walton's puberty is horror theme, however, was new during the Y2K era and this Red Riding Hood equals Big Bad Wolf combination fits the solid coming of age progression and lycanthrope twists. Unlike recent in your face horror clichés, there's sexy here without cheap nudity, the handsome blood and gore isn't too gory, and the non-CGI wolf get ups are well done. The sharp editing isn't hectic or seizure inducing, and the likeable, witty, sardonic characters are given full room to blossom or wax irony—the go to expert on wolfs bane is the town's resident pot dealer! The audience doesn't know how far the scares and suspense will escalate or if this sisterly core can survive the wolfy puberty. Who's the original dang wolf? Yes, this lovely werewolf build up and fine feminine sisterhood feels imbalanced in the end, however this is a great, morbid teen thriller for budding macabre young ladies.

The Innkeepers A lovely, historic atmosphere and setting accent the brooding suspense of this 2011 thinking person's haunted hotel tale, starring Sarah Paxton and Kelly McGillis. The situational scares, ghost investigations, touches of quirky humor, and genuine conversations feel much more realistic than those so-called reality ghost shows. The subtle fears, whiff of gore, and shock scares are quality, but the what you don't see whispers, overnight isolation, unknown paranormal activity, and psychic reactions are better. The simple lack of a camera and reliance on EVP gear for the onscreen investigation forces the audience to pay attention. While some modern viewers may dislike the slow burn pace or find the unambitious characters annoying, the lack of easy explanations and typical boobalicious scream queens is refreshingly honest.

Lady Frankenstein I'm not normally a fan of classic film star Joseph Cotton, but his blend of grave robbing, unethical desperation, and father/daughter compassion is perfect for this 1971 Italian twist on the Shelley theme. "Man's will be done," Cotton says, but it is Rosalba Neri doing the titular monstrous mayhem, evil deeds, and uniquely saucy spins instead of just being the cliché horror victim or resurrected bride. Ethical debates about money, man, and God accentuate dialogue of radical Victorian science and a woman's place in the medical profession. The gothic mood, snow, and firelight work wonderfully with the cool mad scientist laboratory—complete with clockworks, bubbling Rube Goldbergs, and perfectly timed thunder and lightning, of course. Unfortunately, there are various editions in need of a proper restoration—including an edited 85 minute print in the public domain. Perhaps this isn't as depraved as we might expect nowadays and a little too quick toward the finale, but this macabre period delight is worth the pursuit.

Let's Scare Jessica to Death This hour and a half from 1971 doesn't feel PG-13 thanks to askew camera angles, bent up-close shots, bizarre suggestion, tension, and innuendo. The simple tunes and steady beats make for a quiet, eerie orchestration. Toss in a hearse, fall leaves, grave rubbings, female apparitions, empty rocking chairs on abandoned porches, hippie vagrants, séances, and the mood is set! The narration, however, is a little dry. The immediate unreliability and suspect nature is fine—she was "away" veiled mental institution talk and all that—but the inner monologue feels redundant thanks to the sleepy inlet setting and already established atmosphere. Early 70s stylings and more historical decor and accessories accentuate the fear and isolation far better, even if the brief yuppie sing-along is dated. Zohra Lampert is a little annoying and flaky as our titular would be victim to start, but her fears become a worthwhile anchor as the proverbial plot thickens and the jump scares increase thanks to freaky townsfolk, evil history, and morbid antiques. No one wants to say things like crazy, supernatural, ghosts, or vampire, which makes for some confusion or deduction that today's spoon-fed audiences might not be used to doing. Granted, the title is also misleading; the scares here may seem like all the obvious, cliché staples, too. Thankfully, the lack of nudity, little blood, and disturbing water scares make for a very effective, well-paced, thinking person's serious horror picture.

Lights Out I like short films and wish they got more mainstream attention and recognition, but I don't think I've ever reviewed something this short at under three minutes. I can talk longer than this is! However, director David F. Sandburg's winner of the Bloody Cuts Horror Challenge 2013 starring Lotta Losten got me. Not many purportedly scary films these days can capture this unseen suspense, the increasing infringement of the unknown in the sanctity of the home, bedroom, and childhood under the covers safety. If bigger industry names or Hollywood studios don't notice Sandburg and this smartly simplistic viral sensation, they should certainly take note at the taut tension and straightforward filmmaking. Yes.

Mama Jessica Chastain and Nikolaj Coster-Waldau lead this 2013 scary fairy tale from producer Guillermo Del Toro, director Andres Muschietti and co-writers Barbara Muschietti and Neil Cross. Dangerous snowy roads, car action, and police radio immediately establish the isolated cabin and wooded perils for these adorable little girls and their innocent statements. Firelight only scenes, dark surroundings, and creepy noises accent the almost livable but messy designs and wild child state of mind. Eerie observation rooms, case study reports, medical analysis, and research montages anchor the scary amid a reality of courtrooms, technology, and red tape. Some of the brighter colors do seem too pretty or oversaturated; however, pleasing shadows, reflections, and flicking lights keep the spooky subtle. Megan Charpentier and Isabelle Nelisse create an excellent mix of sympathy and disturbing—their child artwork, whispers, and games are both cute and eerie along with moth symbolisms and leaf motifs. Psychiatrist Daniel Kash is right when he tells Chastain to grow up, but he also foolishly doesn't share all his case findings. Is this film about a doctor and a woman trying to help in this unique child tale or is it about scaring the obligatory but rocker babe? Longtime horror viewers won't be fooled by the surprising moments and twists here, but fortunately, there is enough child likability and ghostly traditional style for a disturbing watch or two.

The Resident I didn't like the last Hilary Swank horror attempt _The Reaping_—actually I dislike any time she goes off her Oscar winning type cough—P.S. I Love You—cough. Thankfully, she's solid as a strong but socially awkward and somewhat man needy doctor in an ominous apartment for this 2011 nuHammer thriller. Likewise, Jeffrey Dean Morgan is effective, even if it's obvious he's the too-good-to-be true handyman in a horror movie. At the standard 90 minutes, precious time is wasted with cool opening credits—not usually a good sign for a recent horror film—and the story is slow to get going and ultimately quite predictable. The cheating boyfriend explanation for her moving comes a little too late and the color gradient looks over processed, but the hospital blood and gore are well done. Of course, Christopher Lee has a great introduction. He looks like a perfectly respectable grandfather, yet there's something just a bit creepy old man about him, and I love it!

The Sentinel A big name cast and lots of familiar faces—including Chris Sarandon, Eli Wallach, Jerry Orbach, Beverly D'Angelo, Burgess Meredith, Jeff Goldblum, Christopher Walken, John Carradine, Ava Gardner, Arthur Kennedy, and hey look it's Tom

Berenger and Nana Visitor—appear in this 1977 pseudo-satanic thriller. Although I've never heard of model turned actress Cristina Raines and her undefined training is apparent in some scenes, her confused woman is very likeable and holds the picture together as the unexplained events, bizarre dreams, suspect mental issues, and suicidal baggage intensify. Complex blends of religious iconography, nighttime scares, and plenty of twists and twisted-ness create some fine subterfuge. The fantastic NYC locations mix wonderfully with a suspiciously unsuspicious Old World look and feel, too. Yes, some scenes are silly and there might be some iffy plot holes. However, toss in some kinky nudity and devilish debauchery with the evil plots, and the demented atmosphere here remains entertaining throughout.

Spider Baby Talk about an awkward dinner table! Lon Chaney Jr. sings the catchy little song matching the opening cartoon titles of this bizarre 1964 family cannibalism tale written and directed by Jack Hill. Although the introduction seems slow to start, the ominous drive to the decrepit Victorian house, crazy knife killings, and cut off ears establish the twistedness. Quirky beatnik music, mellow pace, and low quality black and white photography belie the increasing suspense as those incoming ruthless cousins explore the house at their own peril. Our older, aged Creighton with the sweet heart seems like a reasonable, loyal caregiver yet he's harboring a trio of seriously demented killers. The titular Jill Banner and her sister Beverly Washburn would seem to live quietly in peace, so long as no kids hop their fence or mailmen knock on their door that is. Internal references to classic horror film clichés and *The Wolf Man* add to this witty whiff of comedy, but veiled statements about trying not to be bad, being unable to help one's behavior, or possibly not knowing any better perfectly contrast the humor and the ironic, supposedly normal but snotty and infiltrating rival family branch. Society vilifies the sick or ill it can't understand, and the contorted and creepy to see yet innocent and tragic Sid Haig initially has our sympathies. Of course, when the disturbia turns kinky, we know why these people remain under lock and key. Along with the scandalous inbreeding, cannibalism, family murder, black garter belts, and intriguing commentaries, the not for the feline faint of heart scene, eerie dumbwaiter uses, crawling spiders, and the general dementedness of seeing older people act like evil kids, sets the bar for future macabre domestic horror pictures.

__Triangle__ Director Christopher Smith creates a great, mind-bending and smartly head-scratching ride in this watery 2009 Bermuda triangle thriller. There are a few scares, but the within storytelling and multi-level camera work develop more of a thinking viewer's *Twilight Zone* heavy before full on gore or modern slasher horror. A decrepit and sinister ship, carefully placed mirrors, dual appearances and deceptions, and altered audience perceptions layer the plotting and paths for desperate mother Melissa George. Although "It" boy Liam Hemsworth is iffy, his role is relatively small. Hefty concepts, time twists, and intelligent debate outshine any small scale productions here, too. I'd like to say more, but I don't want to spoil anything!

__Vampyres__ Late Spanish director Jose Ramon Larraz gets right to the unabashedly naked lesbian soft-core action and slobbery kisses for this 1974 blood and spicy flick. Despite our contemporary love of sex sex sex, one might initially groan at this potentially unnecessary boobs before violence, yet the kitschy mood and sensuous gothic tone works with the blended British seventies style and Old World, cluttered Victorian creepy. Outside of some great cars and sparse electricity, the viewer may not know when this takes place, and the Oakley Court estate and churchyards are perfectly isolated eerie. Couple Sally Falkner and Brian Deacon give the audience a likeable believer and a relatable skeptic to set up scares and shocks while Murray Brown learns the dangers of picking up beautiful hitchhikers in dark capes Marianne Morris and Anulka Dziubinska. Though the foul afoot is certainly suspected, the simmering, alluring build doesn't reveal the juicy all at once. Sure, some plot points don't make much sense and the seventies sex and kinky lingerie strip teases can be laughable, I grant you. However, the strong titillation provides comfort, rough, or bemusement ahead of the bloody kickers. The predatory approach is traditional but there are no fangs and quick, demented, near cannibalistic feminine twists keep the pace unconventional. Viewers who prefer their gore, language, and sex fast and furious may find the action slow or the plot lame, but the meant to be hazy and dreamy mood belies an intense finish.

What's the Matter with Helen? Debbie Reynolds—America's fifties sweetheart, the mother of Princess Leia—in a scary movie? Oh yes! I'm not exactly a Shelly Winters fan, for she always seems so frumpy and annoying. However, that stuffy works for writer Henry Farrell and director Curtis Harrington here. We know it is wrong, and these broads aren't exactly kosher, yet there's something about watching old ladies get terrorized onscreen. The diverging juxtapositions of the toe tapping, Hollywood star struck Reynolds and increasingly reclusive, paranoid Winters is quite genius. Simple delights such as early newsreels, radio broadcasts, and early prank phone calls add an extra accent to gruesome crime scene photos, great Depression era cars, and stunning styles to enchant any fashionista. Sweet jazzy tunes like "Goody Goody" are surprisingly perfect for a horror picture; recitals and almost musical sequences further pull the viewers out of the expected scary genre comfort zone, too. Although "Oh, You Nasty Man" performed by a little girl is just a bit too creepy. It's funny to see vintage crazy stage moms, dolling them up in great hats and frocks that don't change their stripes! The photography is a rich, classic, almost antique or patina palette of colors, and the Depression period really makes this 1971 picture stand out. Today's teen slashers-fed audiences don't expect to see sophisticated scares in this time or place, and it adds to the unsettling feelings onscreen. Classic audiences, fans of the period, or those just looking for a unique, subliminally scary picture will be entertained here.

Whatever Happened to Baby Jane? We can't imagine anyone but Bette Davis and Joan Crawford in a sibling rivalry this extreme! The two Oscar winners (_Jezebel_ and _Mildred Pierce_, respectively) finally clash onscreen in this 1962 adaptation from director Robert Aldrich. The introductory rise thru the show business eras, fun vaudeville tunes, vintage film reels, swift editing, period clothing, cool cars, and plenty of suspense all cap off the warped drama and black and white demented nostalgia. De Vol's over the top yet on form and fitting music adds to the fun weirdness of seeing the slovenly done up Davis. Perhaps we tend to think of her as so nice and grandmotherly today—unlike Crawford. Thanks to the likes of _Mommie Dearest_, it's a little ironic to see her as Ms. Sympathy. And yet…both ladies put our expectations on end, and it's a tough call on who is the better performer. Although the shock moments are probably well known now, the audience wonders how far off the deep end the wonderfully cruel and simplistic scares will go. There's great, bemusing trepidation in the little things we take for granted in the 21st century—getting a letter to a neighbor, not knowing what's for dinner, leaving the phone off the hook. Minds, mirrors, twisted selves—the unraveling of this relationship train wreck is quite horrific—or at the very least criminal! Where is the desperation greatest? Who's more deserving of their internal hostage via the wheelchair or the childlike mind? This staple is perfect for classic film fans, fans of the cast, and anyone looking for a sophisticated feminine horror spin.

Downright Horror
by Mary Abshire

My interest in horror, Sci-Fi, and paranormal started when I was a young kid. One of my favorite movies is the classic version of *Halloween*. I can watch it repeatedly without getting bored. The music is awesome and so fitting with the movie. I do so enjoy John Carpenter's works.

Today though, when I watch *Halloween*, it doesn't frighten me. When I was younger, the idea of some psycho on the prowl during Halloween did spook me. Not so much today and I don't know why, but I still enjoy the movie. Come on, it's a classic.

There is one movie that scared me when I was a kid and still freaks me out. In fact, I refuse to watch it. Can you guess what it is?

It's *The Exorcist*. The story of a young girl being possessed just freaks me out. Possession is real. Yeah, serial killers are real too, but at least we can fight them. Watching an innocent girl possessed just... I can't watch. The voice, the spewing, the head turning, the jabbing of the cross, the crawling on the ceiling... No, no, no. I try to tell myself it's just a movie with special effects. Well, yeah, but I'm betting possession is pretty close to all of that. The worst of hell in your body. No thanks, I'll pass.

Another movie that spooked me was *Event Horizon*. Sam Neil is one of the best actors to play in horror movies. Again, sound effects made the movie more intense and frightening. I rarely watch the movie, yet I recommend it.

In my opinion, there are various degrees of horror. Off the top of my head, the gross, the disturbing, the special effects, the supernatural, and the downright evil.

Special effects and gross horror go hand in hand sometimes. I think of the *Saw* movies. They're not frightening at all, to me. I do like them as they are creative, but they definitely are gross due to the special effects. *Creepshow* and the first/original *A Nightmare on Elm Street* rank high on the gross list. I also like *Death Proof* and *Planet Terror* by Quentin Tarantino. While there isn't much horror, I'd put those two movies on my gross list, and I love them. I love the originality of the stories.

Disturbing horror movies would include the *Serpent and the Rainbow*, directed by Wes Craven, and the new version of *Halloween*. The new version of *Halloween* portrays Michael as a warped kid from birth. I find it scary because what we see in the movie really happens to kids today. It's a good movie, but disturbing. Also on my disturbing movie list is *The Silence of the Lambs* and *Hannibal Rising*. I absolutely love *Hannibal Rising*. The movie shows how Dr. Lector struggled from a small child to adulthood and became a skilled killer. It's an excellent movie and one of my favorites.

Supernatural is my favorite category, from *The Hunger* to *Let the Right One In* (not the American version *Let Me In*) I love vampire movies. Didn't care so much for *Interview with the Vampire*. It was just ok, in my opinion. I love Anne Rice books, just not the movies. One of my favorite supernatural movies is *American Werewolf in London*. It would fall into my gross list too. When the guy changes…OMG. Great effects and his ghostly friend is cool, though gross.

A less frightening movie I highly recommend is *The Orphanage*. It doesn't involve supernatural creatures. Well, except for ghosts. Guillermo del Toro produced the movie and filmed it in Spanish. The story is great as well as the special effects.

I also enjoy apocalyptic horror movies. Struggling to survive after major catastrophes (or fighting zombies) makes for great horror movies. *28 Days Later* and movies like *Return of the Living Dead* come to mind.

Paranormal type movies are decent, though not as horrific in my opinion. I'm a long time *X-Files* fan. Movies with aliens or ghosts are good to watch any day of the week.

In case you haven't noticed, I enjoy a wide range of horror movies. 1980's horror flicks rank high on my lists. I like to think I'm a very open-minded person, but when it comes to the downright evil movies, I have to pass. (Unless it's *Devil* by M. Night Shyamalan.)

Horror movies have been a part of my life since I was a child. Did they influence me? Sure, but not in the wrong kind of way. I'm no killer. Horror flicks showed me a dark world full of mystery, pain, and challenges. There are bad guys and struggles of good versus evil. Some of the bad guys are not so bad, just misunderstood. No, I'm not talking about the killers, I'm referring to vampires. I love the bloodsuckers. And while I'm not a fan of demons, I like to write and read about them. Why? Because I love the struggle of good versus evil (the good winning of course). Instead of scaring me away, horror movies opened my mind to a world of possibilities. To all the horror producers, directors, writers, I commend you. Thank you for sharing your creativity with us.

keeping amish country bloody

by Kristin Battestella

Greetings addicts! Kbatz here getting my gore on with Mike Lombardo of Reel Splatter Productions, an independent film team based outside Lancaster, Pennsylvania.

Kbatz: Evening Mike! Tell us addicts, how did a splatter film studio find its way to Amish Country? How long have you been making movies?

Mike: Well, I was born and raised in this concrete jungle known as Lancaster county. When most people hear Lancaster, PA, they think farms and horse and buggy drive by shootings, but the part of the county I live in is fairly boring suburbs, just outside the city. It sounds strange, but this area is actually a great place for filmmaking. I've been making weird little splatter flicks in my backyard since I was a kid and I officially started Reel Splatter Productions about ten years ago. Since then, things have obviously grown into much larger and complex projects and I now do a fair amount of FX work on other people's productions, but I still love it here in Bumfuck, PA. There are lots of cool locales to shoot in and I've been lucky enough to band together with some fellow weirdoes that like to play with fake blood too. I would not be able to do it without them, and I don't think I could find a better crew anywhere else in the world! Besides, if you look at some of the indie splatter greats like Sam Raimi and Peter Jackson, they came from small little suburban towns like mine. Something about being surrounded by ultra-conservative, close-minded assholes really gets the creative juices flowin'.

Kbatz: You mix up the blood and comedy, but also promise weird and necrophilia extremes. How do you find a balance between the humor and hardcore?

Mike: Haha, I don't. I pretty much just write whatever pops into my head and I let it exist as it does. I have a really bizarre sense of humor and I write what I would like to see on screen. Someone once told me that a short I had made, *Where Has All The Laughter Gone?* which is a sort of art house parody that has a depressed clown shooting himself, made them feel guilty for laughing. I think that sort of became a subconscious goal of mine since then. I love the juxtaposition of the goofy and grotesque. There's nothing I enjoy more than skewing the tone of a movie by mixing a scene of hardcore violence with totally inappropriate comedy. It keeps the audience off balance and they end up laughing uncomfortably as someone gets their neck hacksawed open so deep, it opens like a Pez dispenser. It's really wonderful sitting in a crowd at a film festival and seeing the looks of confusion and laughter/disgust on people's faces as they see some of this stuff. They have no idea how to react to what they're seeing. I mean, I think it's completely okay to laugh at this kind of stuff, it's not real. It's rubber and corn syrup. It's all for fun and I want people to have a good time. I'm not trying to give anyone nightmares for the rest of their life.

Kbatz: Your website warns those easily offended not to proceed thanks to all forms of sick stuff, yet you also promise no nudity. Why not? Where is the line of exploitation or going too far in a production?

Mike: That little warning bit was actually a riff on the ad campaign for one of my all-time favorite movies, *Lucio Fulci's Zombi*. It said that the film contains scenes of graphic violence and gore, but no explicit depictions of sex. I always thought it was kinda funny and I am in love with 70's exploitation film ads. Plus, at the time of writing it, it was fairly accurate. The thing is, there will be some very graphic nudity coming up in a short film called *Charnel House*. It's a necrophilia love story and it contains a fair amount of nudity, both male and female. I don't have any problem with nudity or sex in a movie as long as it serves a purpose, I don't like nudity for the sake of nudity. I feel the same way about violence and gore. As long as it serves the story I don't think there is a line to cross. A good example is *A Serbian Film*. An absolutely morally reprehensible and sickening movie that depicts things I never thought I would ever see on film. I think it's brilliant and I don't consider it exploitation in the least bit. Everything they showed was completely necessary to the narrative and it served a purpose in the story. It never got to the point of gratuitous and I felt like it was as tastefully done as it possibly could be while still showing it. There is certainly a line that you can cross into exploitation and that's a fine line I try to keep in mind. Sometimes it suits the scene but it's very easy to go too overboard with a gore scene or a sex scene. It becomes boring. The audience becomes desensitized and it ceases to have an effect on them.

Khatz: Which comes first, the artistic idea and story or the special effects and creative gore? Do you think of a great use for a chainsaw and build a film around it or is it the other way around?

Mike: It really depends on the project. Most of my ideas come in random fragments while I'm slaving away at my pizza shop day job. It could be a cool death scene or a random joke or even a title that pops into my head. I scribble it down on an order slip and put it in my pocket for later use. I have certainly written movies around FX scenes, but generally I think of a cool concept or storyline and then figure out the gore (if any) depending on where the story goes. Sometimes there will be a new technique or FX set piece that I really want to experiment with, so I'll figure out a way to incorporate it into the script.

Khatz: What's this I hear about bathrooms and pizza mixing with Lovecraft for your latest project The Stall?

Mike: I am a huge fan of H.P. Lovecraft. "Pickman's Model" is one of my favorite short stories and I grew up watching all of the Stuart Gordon/Brian Yuzna Lovecraft movies. I also have an unhealthy obsession with tentacles, so it was only a matter of time before I ended up doing a Lovecraft movie. *The Stall* is the latest and most technically challenging short I've ever done. It's about a young pizza shop employee who ends up trapped in a public restroom during the Lovecraftian apocalypse. It has lots of tentacles and slime and a splash of bitter food service satire. We actually filmed a section of it at the pizza shop I work at so it took on a strange meta quality for me during the production. It was a grueling shoot, the bulk of it was shot in the winter and we were lying on an ice cold concrete bathroom floor in an old factory covered in blood and ultra-slime for seventeen hours at a time with no heat and no sleep. I mean that's pretty standard for a Reel Splatter shoot, and I am lucky to have a totally gung ho crew of maniacs working with me or none of it would be possible. I'm surprised no one got pneumonia! We're finishing up the post production now and it should be out on DVD and playing at film festivals very soon.

Kbatz: How did you get the nickname Dr. Chud? What's the appeal of low budget, bad, 80s horror anyway, and why do you want to make films in that vein?

Mike: The name Dr. Chud came from another of my all time favorite movies (at the time of this writing, I believe I have about 168.5 favorite movies of all time), *C.H.U.D.* A wonderful slice of 80's cheese about urban decay and sewer dwelling homeless people mutating into flesh hungry monsters. That combined with my love of old creature feature hosts spawned the name Dr. Chud. I created a character that wore a gas mask and a trench coat and spent his time foretelling the apocalypse on a cardboard sign and I gave him the name and he became our mascot/logo. I ended up with the nickname because I always play him and he sort of became a symbol of my creative alter ego. At the time of his creation, I was unaware that one of the many revolving members of the punk band The Misfits (a band of which I am not a fan) was also named Dr. Chud. It has caused some confusion in the past, but the two are completely unrelated.

The appeal of bad 80's movies is hard to pinpoint. I think what attracted me to them as a kid was just the sheer outrageousness of them. They all kind of have this "out there" quality and that gives them a certain personality and heart that is lacking in most films. I love the "anything goes" mentality of them and I really want to capture that sense of fun in my own work. The practical FX (however cheesy) also always fascinated me and was a great source of inspiration.

Kbatz: What are your goals for Reel Splatter? Do you hope to remain indie or make it big? What do you hope your viewers take away from your films?

Mike: My only goal for Reel Splatter is to keep making movies and entertaining folks. It's never been about getting big or making money. I just love playing with fake blood and making people laugh. If I have to do that with my last $50 from the pizza shop and not eating for a few days or if I have studio backing and I have millions to spend, the attitude and dream is the same. John Carpenter summed it up perfectly once on the set of *They Live*. He said "When it stops being fun, we stop doing it."

Kbatz: Where can our fellow horror addicts watch your films or find you online?

Mike: You can check out our DVD *Suburban Holocaust: Reel Splatter Volume 1* and the upcoming DVD of *The Stall* at www.ReelSplatter.com

Kbatz: Thanks for taking the time out to chat with HorrorAddicts.net, Mike!

Mike: Thanks for letting me ramble! Keep it REEL folks!

Tomb Toons
and Kid's Horror

by Steven Rose Jr.

Some of you may be wondering what place kids' shows have in a book specializing in horror, which is traditionally a teen and adult genre. Actually, horror films have inspired children's television for decades.

Are some of you old enough to remember those cartoons and live-action kids' shows that were inspired by horror movies? Do you remember the *Real Ghostbusters* cartoon from the 1980s? If you're old enough to remember back even further, into the middle '70s, you may know that those weren't really the real *Ghostbusters* as the cartoon series' title indicates. In 1975 the real, and therefore original, *Ghostbusters* was a live action kids' show that, instead of involving four men and a slime pouring ghost, actually involved only two vaudeville-like men and a gorilla that assisted them on their paranormal missions. Some of you may be saying, that was a cartoon in the 1980s. Well you're right, because when the *"Real"* *Ghostbusters* tried taking the Saturday morning spotlight and they succeeded, the original series was revived as a cartoon in competition, only it was bumped to afterschool hours, for syndicated television.

Let's backtrack a few years from the original *Ghostbusters* Saturday morning series. There was *The Funky Phantom* in (1971), a *Scooby Doo*-like mystery cartoon series involving a group of detective-like teens and their 18th century ghost friend. Then around the same time there was *The Groovy Ghoulies*, a cartoon series based on the three most famous monsters of film, Frankenstein's Monster (Franky), Count Dracula (Drac) and the Wolf-Man (Wolfie) and their many friends and relatives who all dwelled in a haunted castle called Horrible Hall. This series was actually a spin-off from another dark supernatural lore inspired cartoon series—*Sabrina the Teenage Witch* (1969) (itself a spin-off from *The Archies*).

Another kids' show inspired by the three famous movie monsters was actually a live-action series called *The Monster Squad* (1976). In this series, a computer geek-law student, who works in a wax museum, brings the sculptures of Frankenstein's Monster, Dracula and the Wolfman to life and they fight crime together. *The Addams Family* cartoon was also aired in the early '70s. The same year that *Monster Squad* premiered, the producers of live-action kids' shows, Sid and Marty Kroft, came out with a series called *Dr. Shrinker*. The series was about a mad scientist and his dwarvish assistant who shrink a group of island-marooned young adventurers and are after them to perform dangerous experiments on the adventurers.

Moving forward to 1978, the same producers of *Dr. Shrinker* came out with another live-action series called *Horror Hotel*, which involved many of the strange characters from the Kroft brothers' 1969 *Puff 'N Stuff* (an Oz-/Wonderland-like fantasy series). The characters were, a witch named Witchy Poo, a stupid bat named just that–Stupid Bat, a mad scientist owl by the name of Dr. Blinkey, a yellow spider-like monster, a vulture and a green faced magician (from another earlier Kroft series called *Lidville*). They were the staff of a haunted hotel who had a different strange guest each week ("guest" as in both guest star and hotel guest).

The following year, 1979, the *New Flinstones* show came out with some characters who were neighbors to the Neanderthal comic family, the Frankenstones. The patriarchal head of this ghoulish family was a Neanderthal Frankenstein's monster. That same year premiered a cartoon based on the Dracula character, Count Quackula, about a vampire duck who, unlike most of the cartoon monsters we've been talking about, was not a very nice guy—or, rather, ghoul.

As we move into the '80s two more horror-inspired cartoon series came out on Saturday mornings: *Drac Pack* and *Ding Bat and Friends*. *Drac Pack* involved three teenagers: one who was a descendent of Frankenstein's monster, another a descendent of Dracula, and one of the Wolf-Man. Like the characters in *Monster Squad*, these teens also fought crime, only in their case it was up against the same group of villains each week—Dr. Dread and his evil crew of monsters. *Ding Bat* was a more slapstick kind of cartoon involving a vampire dog (Dingbat), a cranky jack-o-lantern, and a skeleton who wore a toilet plunger for a hat.

I already mentioned some of the cartoon series of the latter half of the 1980s such as the two *Ghostbusters* cartoon series. But also, in 1988, the comedian Martin Short came out with his own Saturday morning kids' show that was partly live-action and partly animated. In one of the live action weekly skits, a Dracula-like vampire told horror stories to his child audience, the stories themselves being animated. As the decade came to a close, the *Beetlejuice* movie franchise produced a Saturday morning cartoon series based on the movie's characters.

In the 90's, when the cable television-based *Tales from the Crypt* became popular on syndicated television, a cartoon version came out on Saturday mornings. A new *Addams Family* cartoon series also aired. Then R.L. Stine's kids' horror novel series,

Goosebumps, was adapted for a live-action syndicated series.

In the 2001's Cartoon Network aired *The Grim Adventures of Billy and Mandy*, a series about two kids who are friends with the Grim Reaper. Will there be more horror genre inspired cartoons and kids' shows? The horror genre has become more popular than ever with young people's series of novels such as *Twilight*; TV series such as *True Blood*, *Ghost Whisperer* and *Supernatural*; and big screen movies such as *Paranormal Activity*. How can there not be any horror inspired cartoons and live-action kids shows? Let's hope some will premiere soon enough. Any animators out there in the audience?

READING HORROR

nightshade on Reading

This is a hard section for me because there is a lot of literature out there that is really scary. You will find seven articles here from people that love to read scary stories. Of course, not everyone is scared of the same thing. Some people might find vampires scary while others don't. There are also people who read horror because they are intrigued by the beauty of the settings like in Anne Rice's *Vampire Chronicles*. We all love horror for different reasons, but primarily people read horror to get a good scare.

Sadly, there are no articles here that talk about the scariest books of all. I'm talking about school text books. What kid in school hasn't been scared by looking at a 500 page science book or even worse, a math book. And the price you pay for those heavy tomes is even scarier. Talking about the horror of educational text books is probably way too scary to talk about in this book. I mean, quadratic equations? Molecular composition? Government? *Shiver.* Maybe we should just move on to the section on reading. After all, the *Horror Addicts Guide to Life* is the only textbook us horror addicts will ever need.

it came from the library

by David Watson

Every town has one. A place filled with magic. You can find knights in shining armor, dragons, fairies, space ships, and anything else you can imagine. It's also a place where you can learn about computers, visit foreign lands, and find out someone's life story. For some, it's a place where vampires roam the night, ghosts haunt Victorian homes, and unspeakable creatures wait in the night to kill unsuspecting victims.

I'm talking about your local library. A place where you can find out about anything that interests you. My main passion in life is reading and that passion started in the library. When I was young, I remember my mom taking me to storytime and when I came out, she would have a stack of books for me. I would go home to my favorite blue chair in my room and start reading.

My favorites were books about baseball, super heroes, and of course, horror. Some of the titles I remember from when I was young are, *Georgie The Ghost, The Witch Next Door,* and *The Haunted House.* As I got older I saw my mom reading Stephen King's *The Stand* and I remember thinking I wanted to start reading big scary books for adults. I started with *Salem's Lot* by Stephen King and then went on to Peter Benchley's *Jaws* followed by, Bram Stoker's *Dracula,* Mary Shelley's *Frankenstein,* the works of Clive Barker, and the novelization of the movie *Poltergeist.*

I read other books besides horror, but horror is my favorite genre and I always come back to it. As I got older, hobbies came and went and I got to a point where I didn't like horror films as much, but I never got tired of reading horror. Horror films are more of a collaborative art form and sometimes ideas can get lost in translation. With horror literature, it's more personal. You're reading one person's description of something scary and you're using your imagination to see what they see. It's the theatre of the mind, and what's in your mind is much scarier than anything that can be shown on a movie screen.

Horror movies don't scare me like they did when I was a kid. I still think they're fun to watch, but they don't thrill me anymore. Horror literature, on the other hand, can still scare me. I think in books it's easier to make the reader care about the characters. You can relate to them more because you get to know them on a more personal level and this is what makes horror literature scary. All an author has to do is make the reader care about the character, and then put them in a life threatening situation. A masked serial killer in a book can be scary if I care about his victims, while a masked killer in a movie doesn't always deliver the scares.

Another thing about books is, they make you think. While you're hearing the author's story, you may be thinking of a different vision in your head than the author intended. It's like the author is painting a picture for you with words, but what you see may be different than what they see. This is what makes reading so great. You're getting to know the author and the characters on a personal level and how you see something may be totally different then how another reader sees it, or how the author sees it.

Horror literature never gets old for me. I get excited every time I get a new horror novel and I feel sorry for people who don't understand the genre. I think it's because they've seen too many bad horror movies and think horror is silly or just for kids. These people are missing out and all they have to do is take a trip to the library. They may have to search a little, but they will find that horror isn't silly. If willing to look, they will find hundreds of books on vampires, zombies, werewolves, and other unimaginable horrors. All of them have a different twist on an old idea and they will introduce you to characters that have stared death in the eye, and lived to tell the tale.

A love of horror starts at your local library. The books are waiting...watching...daring you to read them. And daring you to sleep with the lights off.

Top 10 Horror Manga
by Emerian Rich

1. *Death Note* by Tsugumi Ohba & Takeshi Obata
2. *Black Butler* by Kaori Yuki
3. *Godchild* by Kaori Yuki
4. *Rozen Maiden* by Peach-Pit
5. *Tarot Cafe'* by Park Sang-sun
6. *Black Bird* by Kanoko Sakurakoji
7. *Vampire Knight* by Matsuri Hino
8. *Rosario + Vampire* by Akihisa Ikeda
9. *Haunted House* by Mitsukazu Mihara
10. *Murder Princess* by Sekihiko Inui

why i write
post-apocalyptic horror

by Jeff Carlson

I think we're programmed for hardship. In my experience, human beings are happiest when they're working themselves to the bone. Call me crazy, but from what I've seen, people are more likely to feel adrift and unsatisfied when they have too much leisure time. Purpose is the greatest gift. Obstacles are good.

Here's why. For hundreds of thousands of years, life was brutal. It still is for a good chunk of the planet. The technology and wealth we enjoy in North America is a very new development in history, and I think we miss the challenges of day-to-day survival in our comparatively easy modern lives. Some people will even create problems if they have none.

Everyone's had a psychotic girl or boyfriend, right? Well, lots of 'em really are just nut-flavored bologna. They have a neurochemical imbalance or ate too many paint chips as a kid... but some people look for drama and emotional upheaval for reasons they can't explain themselves, reenacting the shortcomings, chaos, or abuse of their childhoods.

Surprise. These drama kings and queens might be exactly the kind of person you'd want at your back during the zombie apocalypse or the aftermath of a comet strike. Each of our nut-flavored friends is a sponge. They're ready to soak up as much trauma as anyone can dish out. They have the stamina, heart, and depth to keep on slogging through the radioactive bugs even long after the last shotgun shell is gone.

They're not the only ones. I like to think I'm the kind of guy you'd give the keys to the bomb shelter and I'm extremely boring and normal—wife, kids, mortgage, bleh—except to say that I grew up fascinated with books like *Lucifer's Hammer* and *The Stand*.

We like to be scared because we have a huge capacity for fear. The most basic element of storytelling is conflict because we respond to it.

For me, writing post-apocalyptic novels isn't so much about exploding helicopters and fifty megaton doomsday bombs as it is about the pleasure of dealing with the best of everything that makes us human: cleverness, grit, loyalty, and self-sacrifice.

Sure, the hot-sex-with-our-last-breath and the gunfights are fun, too, but ultimately my novels boil down to the ability of some people—the greatest of us—to overcome nearly any hurdle. I back my heroes into corners just to watch them wiggle free.

People are tough. We're evolved for less food; more exercise; less sleep; less security; more paranoia. The irony is that we're so good at what we do. We strive for more food; less exercise; more sleep; more security; less paranoia—and we've succeeded.

Look around. Humankind has remade the entire face of the planet, blanketing Earth with electrical grids, highways, super-agriculture, shipping lanes and aircraft, even wrapping the sky in satellites. It's easy to complain about your bills or morning traffic or the neighbor's neglected, ever-barking dogs (you know who you are), but these are fantastic problems to have.

The grocery stores are loaded. We have the industrial strength to roll off three cars per household. Every other family has enough money to spare to feed two dogs and a cat even though they don't have any inclination to walk Sparky and Spot every day and choose instead to leave their canines to noisily go insane, each set of dogs fenced off inside their own isolated little patch of suburbia.

Anyone with the basic education and spare cash to buy this book is richer than 99.99% of the human beings who've ever lived, and yet we can't help imagining what things would be like if we had to start over. Nuclear Armageddon. Superflu. The living dead. Nanotech.

Give me a wild scenario and some smart good guys and I'm happy—just so long as the lights stay on and there's iced tea in the fridge. I'd really rather not be sifting through the rubble for canned food and medicine while we keep one eye peeled for roving gangs of illiterate cannibals.

african american horror writers

by David Watson

A couple of years ago on the HorrorAddicts.net blog, I did an article on African American Horror Writers. February is African American History month and I thought it would be cool to celebrate by showcasing Horror Writers. This blog post got such a big response that I did a part two the next year. I got so many comments on the blog from writers and readers that I wanted to include a list of some of the authors from those two blog posts. There are many great African American Horror writers out there and below you will find a few authors that you'll hopefully want to read in the future.

☠ **L.A. Banks** was born in Philadelphia. She has written in multiple genres and won many literary awards. She is the author of *The Vampire Huntress Series*, which includes twelve novels, one graphic novel and a YA novel. Some critics have called her work: "fresh, hip, fantastic and far superior to Buffy." L.A. Banks has also written a series of six werewolf novels called *The Crimson Moon Series* and is the co-founder of The Liar's Club, a networking group for professionals in publishing and other aspects of entertainment. Sadly, L.A. Banks died of adrenal cancer in 2011.

☠ **Maurice Broaddus** was born in London, England. He graduated from Purdue University and is a senior writer for HollywoodJesus.com. Maurice has written in several genres, his horror novels include: *Devil's Marionette* and *The Knights of*

Breton Court: King Maker. Maurice now lives in Indianapolis, Indiana and is part of the Indiana Horror Writers Association.

☠ **Brandon Massey** was born in Waukegan, Illinois in 1973 and has published three novels a year since 1999. Brandon loved watching horror movies growing up and is a life-long reader. He decided he wanted to start telling his own stories and became a horror writer. Some of his novels include: *Thunderland* and *Covenant*. Brandon has also edited two collections of short stories by African American Horror writers called: *Dark Dreams* and *Voices From The Other Side*: *Dark Dreams 2*.

☠ **Wrath James White** is a former MMA fighter and hard core horror author. In 2011, Wrath wrote a book of dark poetry called *Vicious Romantic* which was nominated for an HWA Bram Stoker award. A movie is in production based on his novel, *The Resurrectionist*. Some of his other works include, *Succulent Prey* and *Population Zero*. Wrath also has a great blog where he talks about politics, religion, and anything else that he finds worthy to talk about.

☠ **Jemiah Jefferson** grew up listening to disco music and watching horror movies. She also loved to daydream and read. She has written non-fiction, erotica, and has written four books in *The Voice of Blood Vampire Series*. Some of her works include *Wounds* and *A Drop of Scarlet*.

☠ **Tananarive Due** is a great science fiction writer that has also written horror. In 2012 Tananarive co-wrote a zombie novel with her husband Steven

Barnes. The book is called *Devil's Wake*, and is set in a post-apocalyptic future where a school bus full of young people try to escape the walking dead and human raiders as society crumbles around them. Tananarive Due is also the writer of *The African Immortals Series* which has been compared to Anne Rice's *Vampire Chronicles*. The storyline is about an Ethiopian sect that traded their humanity to be immortal.

☠ **Andre Duza** is an author who mixes horror, comedy and social commentary. One of his books is called *Dead Bitch Army*, it's about a zombie woman out for revenge during the apocalypse. Another of Andre's novels is *Jesus Freaks* which tells the story of Detective Phillip Makane who woke up to a world of bleeding rain, a homicidal ghost, thousands of zombies, and two men with powers claiming to be Jesus. Andre Duza has also written the hardcore pulp novella about dog fighting and black magic called *Son of A Bitch* with Wrath James White.

☠ **Qwantu Amaru** has a book called *One Blood* which won a 2012 international book award, a National Indie Excellence award, and several other honors. *One Blood* tells the story of Lincoln Baker a man in prison who orchestrates the kidnapping of the governor of Louisiana's daughter. He also resurrects a family curse which goes back to slavery.

So there you have it, a short list of African American horror writers. There are so many excellent authors out there, I hope this list inspires you to find more and keep reading horror. ☠

paranormal bookstore

by Kristin Battestella

Paranormal Books and Curiosities
Bringing the Spirits to the Shore

Tonight Kbatz is chatting with Kathy and the ghostly gang from the Paranormal Books and Curiosities Shop and Museum in Asbury Park, NJ.

Kbatz: Thanks for taking the time to chat it up with HorrorAddicts.net! How did the idea of a paranormal shop come together when you first opened in 2008? Did you find Asbury Park or did Asbury Park find you?

Kathy: I had reached a breaking point in my former career. While I loved what I did, there did not seem to be much forward movement for me doing it. I decided that I could put all of my skills and creativity into something that I was passionate about and my future would then be in my own hands. Of course, I wasn't sure how to do that! I tried a bunch of different approaches, started writing my book, scouted a tour site and ultimately, I decided the time had come for a brick and mortar destination spot for Paranormal enthusiasts and Paranormal Books & Curiosities was born. Asbury park seemed a natural fit, it had a stormy history and it was interesting and unique and I thought Paranormal would fit right in.

Kbatz: Now that 'paranormal' topics are arguably more popular than ever, how do you define your shop and inform against those who would call such themes evil, occult, witchcraft?

Kathy: I find most people who come in are curious, even if they are afraid. I don't consider it my job to convert or convince anyone of anything. I just want people to be able to explore their interests safely. So, when someone comes in an asks me if I am a witch or if I worship the devil (this happens way less frequently than someone asking me if I am psychic or just saying "boo") I tell them the truth, which is I am not, but there are a bunch of books on the front shelves that can help them with any questions they may have about those things!

Kbatz: How do you decide what books, merchandise, equipment, and oddities go in the store? Where do you get your more unusual museum pieces and exhibits?

Kathy: I decide based on my own interest and the interests of my customers. I can tell you that the store I have now is not the one I opened. It is far more diverse than it was in 2008. My customers have helped mold and shape it by the questions they ask. As far as The Paranormal Museum, some items are artists renditions of legends but most relics I have either found in my travels or have been donated to The Paranormal Museum. Many people have objects that are interesting to them, but they feel uncomfortable with them. I am happy to make room for those items and to tell their story.

Kbatz: Do you have a 'curiosity' of which you're most proud?

Kathy: This is tough. I have so many favorites! One of the pieces in The Paranormal Museum that I truly love is a cutting from the Oleander Tree from The Myrtles Plantation. The Myrtles is one of the most famous hauntings in America and it's seminal story concerns a poisoning by oleander from this particular tree. I love the idea that we have the DNA if you will, of a haunting. Speaking of DNA, I also have a strand of Andrew Jackson's hair. Ole Hickory, as he was known, spent a few sleepless nights investigating the

Bell Witch in Tennessee and that earned him a place on our wall.

Kbatz: What's the weirdest object you've come across?
Kathy: Weirdest is tough, because they all make sense once you tell the story…but I do have a Palo Mayombe cauldron complete with bones and blood ash..I suppose some would think that weird.

Kbatz: In addition to book events, you also host psychics, ghost lectures, and weekend ghost tours in the shop and surrounding community. Have you ever been frightened by any encounters? In twenty years in the investigative community, how much legitimate activity have you witnessed? Any false claims or debunkings?
Kathy: I don't know that I have ever been frightened, but certainly I have been made uncomfortable. I consider myself to be quite skeptical, although I don't generally "debunk". I try to explain. "Debunk"-ing implies that there is some kind of hoax or intentional fraud and I don't find that to usually be the case. I have often been able to experience what is claimed by witnesses, but have interpreted my experiences differently than they. I can't put a percentage on it, but I would say that paranormal activity is far more rare than contemporary field enthusiasts (ghost hunters) would have you believe. But it is not nonexistent. There is something that people are experiencing.

Kbatz: How did the Paranormal BC Investigative Team at the store come together?
Kathy: My team came together organically. I get a lot of people asking to join or asking to "come along" on investigations. The truth is, I investigate much less than many other groups because it is very time

consuming and a lot of people who ask for investigations are more curious to see what investigators do than they are concerned that they have activity. Some of my team members came on public investigation and I liked how they approached the subject. It is all about the "fit".

Kbatz: Has the more recent popularity of ghost hunting shows and events helped or hindered the long active investigative community?

Kathy: I think the TV Shows have done both good and bad, but overall I would lean toward good. They have given a broad audience the vocabulary to discuss what we term paranormal. That is good. That helps start and continue conversations. The bad is that they have created an entire army of weekend investigators armed with equipment they only understand from watching TV shows. Is that bad? I don't know. But I know it is frustrating to many people who have been investigating for 15-25 years. Still, I don't see how it has to negatively impact anyone's legitimate research or study. It is annoying for the old school people, but then again, sometimes I think there is a little too much territorialism in general. My recommendation to people interested is what it has always been. Read, learn, read, learn.

Kbatz: How do you deal with any jokesters, non-believers, and other norms who think it's all hooey?

Kathy: I don't mind that, provided they are respectful. I get it. I'm not sure where I sit on these issues myself from day to day. I am always questioning. That is what it means to be a student of something, you question it to learn. That does not mean I tolerate condescension though, or mockery. If you have already made up your mind and are comfortable with what you know or believe, you should have no reason to disrespect other people's journey to their own decision. The key is to be smarter and more articulate than your heckler!

Thanks again, Kathy, for taking the time to scare it up with HorrorAddicts.net! If you are interested in learning more about the book store, go to: www.paranormalbooksnj.com

top 10 book Reviews
by David Watson

10. _Childhood Nightmares Under The Bed_ from Sirens Call publications. It's rare that I read an anthology where I liked every story in it but I did for this one.

9._The Nightmare Project_ by Jo-Anne Russell. This one takes place mostly in an insane asylum which to me makes it terrifying and the main character is excellent the way she goes back and forth from crazy to being a sweet mother who wants to see her kids again.

8. _NightWhere_ by John Everson. This is one bizarre romance that will leave you feeling sick to your stomach.

7. _My Fearful Symmetry_ by Denise Verrico This is a different take on vampires that I really enjoyed.

6. _The Weeping Woman_ by Patricia Santos Marcantonio Good Mexican ghost legend combined with a modern day police thriller.

5. _The Last Adventure of Dr. Yngve Hogalum_ by D.L. Mackenzie. First steampunk tale I've read with a lot of humor. Fun read.

4. _Vaudeville_ by Greg Chapman. I like the concept of traveling side shows so I loved this one.

3._Underwood and Flinch Chronicles Volumes 1 and 2_ by Mike Bennett. Excellent vampire story that I couldn't put down. It's books like this that make me love reading.

2. _Ivory_ by Steve Merrifield. I loved this one. I wasn't sure where it was going until the end. Really good original idea for a book.

1. _Charla_ by Alex Beresford. It's been seven months since I've read this book, even if you take the demon out of the story it still works as a great horror novel.

☠

horror and dark fantasy, one and the same?

by Steven Rose, Jr.

In the last ten years at least, the dark fantasy subgenre has become just about as popular as the horror subgenre. The two have many similar elements even to the point where they may seem interchangeable or synonymous with each other. Dark fantasy has been permeating just about all media, including video games and books. Neil Gaiman is one of the most popular dark fantasy writers of today. J.K. Rowling's *Harry Potter Series* and the TV series *Supernatural* can also be considered to fall under this fantasy subcategory. Authors more associated with strict horror have also written some dark fantasy, like Steven King with his *Dark Tower Series*.

Two other authors, who wrote much science fiction and horror, but also wrote a lot of dark fantasy are Ray Bradbury and Harlan Ellison. Ray Bradbury's most famous dark fantasy is his novel *Something Wicked This Way Comes*, while Ellison has famous stories of the subgenre such as "The Basilisk" and "Chatting with Anubis."

Directors such as M. Night Shyamalan and Guillermo Del Toro, who typically make horror movies, like *Devil* and *The Orphanage*, also make films that can be classified as dark fantasy. It shouldn't be too surprising that such authors and movie directors of horror also produce dark fantasy works since the two subgenres are both imaginative, dark forms of storytelling, but what literary elements and conventions really distinguish the two?

123

Supernatural horror is a subgenre of fantasy because it involves imaginary events such as hauntings and black magic. Horror stories emphasizing more realistic menacing characters, such as serial killers, would not be considered supernatural horror and so would hardly fall under the umbrella of the fantasy genre. So in general, fantasy storytelling, regardless of the medium, involves any type of plot that is centered on magical or impossible events.

Horror stories involve the unknown and mysterious, but these two elements are much more threatening to the individual. They are usually threatening to a character's life either spiritually or physically. Therefore, the threatening force is some sort of unfamiliar being such as a ghost, demon, or vampire, and is often associated with the underworld. Although the term "horror" has primarily referred to a sense of fear for a person's own soul and therefore spiritual life (as is the case with *Dracula*) it has also come to be associated with an extreme fear for one's physical life.

If the threatening being is not of the supernatural realm, then it is often associated with it through superstition. This is the case with *The Phantom of the Opera*. The Phantom is not really a supernatural being himself but, because he hides in obscure parts of the opera house and kills people, he is thought to be a ghostly presence. Throughout the horror narrative, there are many unexpected attacks or pursuits from the monster, often in dark settings, resulting in shock on the audience's part. Needless to say, such evoking of fear plays a crucial role in the horror story.

Often at the end of a horror story, the reader or viewer is left hanging, but not in the sense of a lack of a satisfying conclusion. The audience is left hanging in the sense that they wonder what will happen to the characters' lives after the characters have faced the traumatic situation brought on by the threatening figure or monster. Therefore, the conclusion to a horror story tends not to be as joyful or promising as that of fantasy, and because the story has been focused on the menacing being itself and the terror it has caused, the other characters' lives are not elaborated on in the conclusion making it much shorter than that of the typical fantasy. The monster may have been destroyed by this time or somehow banished from the setting, but what happens to the characters next is anybody's guess. The monster may return, as is the case with many Hollywood horror films (and so why sequels are so popular with them) or the main characters may have post trauma to deal with that may drive them to insanity. Because of these possibilities, the conclusion to the horror story is more realistic than the more fairytale happy ending of the fantasy.

Dark fantasy tends to contain literary elements from both epic fantasy and horror. The dark fantasy plot often involves a quest on the main character's part, but it is often a quest into darker, more forbidden settings. The hero may or may not have friends or companions on that quest with him/her. The obstacles he/she faces are menacing creatures that you find in many horror stories, creatures such as zombies or evil spirits ready to devour the hero either physically or spiritually. There often tends to be more fairy or folk tale elements in this type of story than in horror stories. Therefore, there may be magical creatures, such as fairies or talking animals that help the hero, and the hero may come from humble beginnings like the hero in a fairytale often does. Also, the story's ending is more like that in the fairytale—a joyful ending where everything turns out good for the hero(es) and they either go on living life as normal as before or better.

These distinguishing elements between horror and dark fantasy can best be seen if we compare a horror novel such as *Dracula* with a dark fantasy novel such as Neil Gaiman's *Neverwhere*. In *Dracula*, a young man who can be considered the hero goes on a journey to the evil count's estate in Transylvania on business. He is imprisoned by the count, and faces many obstacles in his attempt to escape and in doing so, is in utmost fear for his life. He finally does escape, but the count follows him home to his native England. It is there where Dracula causes the terror and havoc on not just the hero's, Jonathan Harker's, friends and beloved, Mina, but even on the society at large. The horror of this creature, is that he can take control of a person's life and soul, making them into one of the living dead like himself. He is immortal and undefeatable. He can appear anywhere at any time, and unlike in most of the movie adaptations, can even walk about by day under certain circumstances. He can make people come to him over remote distances by merely thinking about it, like he does with Mina. Jonathan Harker, Mina, and the vampire hunter, Dr. Van Helsing, form a kind of expedition to go after Dracula and kill him after the evil count has fled back to his native Transylvania. In this way, the basic mythic motifs of the quest and battle against an enemy comes up in this novel. But even though Dracula has become a threat to an entire society, the climaxing battle here is more for an individual's soul, Mina's.

Gaiman's *Neverwhere* is a story that is actually developed from the basic plot of Lewis Carroll's *Alice in Wonderland*. The story mostly takes place at night in the underground of London. Because it's based on

Alice in Wonderland, it's got a fairytale quality to it and this kind of otherworld atmosphere, yet it takes place in the subterranean structures of an actual geographical based city. However, this underground world in the novel is a fantastical one in that it is seldom seen by Londoners and is occupied by magical beings and so is an environment of mystery. One of the magical beings is an enchantress who sucks the life source out of people, an element of horror, since it is so close to the idea of sucking the soul out of a person. It is a more personal threat like what we see in *Dracula*, than a societal one. But the very fact that this hidden society comes out both underground and above at night while the rest of Londoners are sleeping, gives the setting a more imaginary, dream-like quality seen in much fantasy. The majority of the characters the hero comes in contact with are of magic and mystery, as opposed to the more rational based human characters in *Dracula* (save for the vampires themselves, of course). So the quest in *Neverwhere*, unlike *Dracula*, involves more fantastical characters who help the hero on his journey. The purpose of the quest is more societal than it is personal.

Comparing these two popular novels, we can see that the distinction between the genres of horror and dark fantasy is that one is more emphasized on the threat of the individual as opposed to a whole society. More specifically, the threat to a person's soul. However, there is a more fairytale quality to the dark fantasy than there is to the horror story since more impossible characters such as talking and humanized animals occur. In the horror story, the characters are more rational and realistic and the plot, although fantastical in its involving supernatural creatures, consists of more realistic and so more believable events.

Another factor that we shouldn't overlook is that the distinction between these two genres is also due to the commercial industry's categorization and marketing of fiction. The majority of book retailers sell their literary merchandise according to popular interests, and therefore according to what the majority of customers are going to be looking for in story type. But in order for retailers to do that, and in order for them to consider readers' preferences, the literary conventions of these story types have to be considered.

So, the distinction between the genres of horror and dark fantasy seem to be based on two factors: literary convention and marketing. What are your thoughts on the differences in these two subgenres? Would you say the two are based more on conventions or more on marketing methods? Are such categorizations more up to the reader than the forces of literary convention and marketing? Are horror and dark fantasy interchangeable terms?

horror music

nightshade on music

When you think of horror music, what is the first thing you think of? Is it "The Monster Mash" by Bobby Boris Pickett? If that's the only thing that comes to mind, you really need to get educated. Here we have some lists and interviews that will get you started on being more knowledgeable on horror and dark music. There are plenty of spooky musicians out there that will fill your horror-loving heart with joy. All you have to do is pick a genre.

You might want to look into horror soundtracks, which include orchestral music you hear in the background of horror movies and music that could be the background of a horror movie but isn't, such as groups like Midnight Syndicate or Shadow's Symphony. There are also other genres like horror Punk (The Misfits), Gothic Rock (The Cure), or Darkwave (Depeche Mode). You can find dark music that can fit anyone's tastes.

I like to record the audio to movies to listen to when I can't watch. I suggest *Dracula* (1931) with Bela Lugosi as your first foray into movie track listening. Knowing the movie as well as we do, you can just picture the carriage going up the hill when you hear that creepy music. Bela's voice is music in itself and with our active horror imaginations, sometimes the movies are spookier without the visuals.

I also like the sounds of screams when people see me walking down the street, but that's just me.

hORROR-fRiendly lOve sOngs

by HorrorAddicts.net

Ah, the horror love song. What do you dedicate to that lovely ghoul or handsome goblin when the time comes to express the inner workings of your heart? When Valentine's Day comes around, do you dread the big heart day or do you welcome it with open arms? Are you dreaming of that dark-clad beauty or are you currently in the arms of said goddess? Are you hoping for a quick fling or staying the hell away from all that lovey-dovey crap?

Well, here are some horror-friendly love songs to dedicate to your love, your ex, or that leather-clad hotty you happen to meet in the club.

1. "This Love" by Pantera: Does your love hurt?

2. "So Close It Hurts" from the *Suck* movie soundtrack: I almost killed you last night... Whoops!

3. "Love Song" by The Cure: Always a classic.

4. "Marry Me" by Emilie Autumn: A rather jaded and beautifully morbid look at marriage.

5. "Army of Love" by Kerli: For all you shiro goths, grab your army, and suit up!

6. "Love You To Death" by Type O Negative: Now that's some hard lovin'.

7. "Let Me Rest In Peace" by Spike from *Buffy the Vampire Slayer*: Ever want your ex to just leave you the fuck alone?

8. "Beneath a Moonless Sky" from *Love Never Dies*, the sequel to *Phantom of the Opera*: For you dark musical buffs... Phantom (monster) love.

9. "Stay" by Shakespeare Sisters: Soulful, sappy, wonderful. Sing it sister.

10. "Temple of Love" by Sisters of Mercy: Love that hard driving sound. ♀

Top old-School Goth SongS
by Emerian Rich

Old-school goth, ah... the words send shivers up my spine. For any of you who were in the goth scene in the 80's and 90's this music holds a special place in your hearts. Clubs with beds plush with red velvet and chains hanging from the ceiling. Industrial light shows mixed with digitized voices and leather. Men in long skirts and bigger hair than the girls. The next morning, raccoon eyes from forgetting to remove your layers of black eyeliner. Some of us still live in this world and the music of that time cannot be forgotten. Some people instantly think of the more popular tracks from bands like The Cure, Nine Inch Nails, Concrete Blonde, and Ministry. Others take the lesser known road with Type O Negative, Christian Death, and Rosetta Stone. Whatever your old school goth road may be, it's a genre you can never forget. Here are my top ten, never to be forgotten (by me at least), old-school goth songs. For those of you who were there—enjoy. For those of you who missed it, you've got some listening to do, baby.

1. **"Vampire's Cry"** by Nosferatu: Sometimes I hear that whisper in my dreams.
2. **"Sugar Babies"** by P. Vampire: I recently had to rip this from the CD because I can't find it anywhere to download, what a loss to the community! LOVE this song about a creepy arsonist man watching suburban ballet girls dance and then burning them up! Morbid, yes, but this song makes it so fun to listen to.
3. **"Paint it Black"** by Mephisto Walz: An anthem for our generation as this goth band remakes the 1966 song by the The Rolling Stones.

4. "Chain" by Switchblade Symphony: The music and vocals on this are just beautiful.

5. "Iron Helix" by Xorcist: Wakes the mutated robot-alien inside me.

6. "Severina" by The Mission UK: This has a special place in my heart because I found it after I wrote Severina, my character from *Night's Knights*. She is such a strong and beautiful woman and this song appeals to the spiritual side of her when Markham and Julien leave her alone at the castle in England. She sort of goes crazy being alone, but this leads to the challenge to create the perfect vampire.

7. "The Days of Swine and Roses" by My Life with the Thrill Kill Kult: "Christians, Zombies, Vampires!" This is me and my husband's "song". It conjures early days at a goth club in San Francisco where we had our first date.

8. "Dr. Jekyll and Mr. Hyde" by The Damned: "Welcome to the underworld..." I love the video for this song because it's in the vampire heyday. I saw them in the 90's and they were much older, but still had that great sound and a sexy new devilgirl guitarist. Worth the wait!

9. "Deception" by Cruxshadows: Love the hair! Something about this song gets under my skin and makes me feel dirty. Analyze that!

10. "Test My Reaction" by Spahn Ranch: Love this song because it's just goofy. This is my happy goth song. If goth had a pop song, this would be it.

Interview with Midnight Syndicate

by Emerian Rich

Midnight Syndicate is the most beloved atmospheric band in our cherished horror genre. They've done everything from Halloween CDs to creating background music for films like *Axe Giant: The Wrath of Paul Bunyan*. They produced their own movie, *The Dead Matter*, in 2010 and even began producing their own live multimedia Halloween concerts in 2014. Midnight Syndicate is composed of Ed Douglas and Gavin Goszka. My favorite thing about Ed and Gavin is that they are horror addicts, just like us. Sure, they love making music, but to them, it's a way of life, a horror perspective that makes creating soundtracks so exciting. I was lucky enough to pull them away from their busy creative lives for an interview.

Emz: How did you guys start Midnight Syndicate?

Ed: It started way back in like 95', 96'. I had this idea of a band that created soundtracks to imaginary films, blending movie score and instrumental music with sound effects. The idea is that, when you put in a Midnight Syndicate album and close your eyes, you are transported to a world or a movie of your own creation. Midnight Syndicate combined what I loved most, the horror genre, the supernatural and instrumental music. Our albums take people on different journeys. It could be a haunted insane asylum, a haunted house, or even a dragon's lair. Our most recent album, *Monsters of Legend*, is a meant to be a journey into the world of the Universal and Hammer Horror films. We want to transport you to a place where Dracula, Frankenstein, and Wolfman could be right around the corner. The album starts with you going to that creepy village in all those movies where the villagers are telling you, "Don't go up to the castle!" But you still do.

Gavin: I met Ed as a customer, actually. I was working in a music store and he came in to build his studio. He was working on a multimedia concert, kind of like a predecessor of what we do at Cedar Point, and I was immediately impressed by a lot of his ideas and his interest in horror. I said, "Hey, if you're ever looking for someone to work with in the future, give me a call." About two months later, he called me and I was on board. It's been great to watch it grow and develop.

Emz: What is the Cedar Point Halloweekends show all about?

Ed: Well, after sixteen years of making these albums, we're finally performing live together. The show is called *Midnight Syndicate Live! Legacy of Shadows* and it's a multimedia concert that blends live music, film, and theatrics. We debuted it at Cedar *Point's* 2014 *HalloWeekends* event and it couldn't have gone better. From working with the team at Cedar Point and our own designers, Screamline Studios, to the filming of the different segments with Robert Kurtzman's Creature Corps and 529 Films, the show ended up as good or better than we originally envisioned. What's most important, the audiences really loved it.. From what people were telling us, it's unlike any other amusement park show they've ever seen. It's certainly set us up to do more shows in more places in the years to come.

Gavin: It's cool because we get people coming out of the show, going back into the show again. They're like, I need to see this again, I didn't catch everything. So there's a lot to look at, there's a lot to catch that you might not always see the first time. It's nice to hear people saying it's really unique and that they didn't expect something like this at a theme park.

Emz: Gavin, don't you have another music project going?

Gavin: I've started a side project called Parlormuse. I've been really into the Victorian era and the culture and everything for awhile now. I'm exploring some of the sheet music that I've been collecting from that period and adapting it for more of a modern audience, using a folk-rock kind of approach. There is one full album out and I am following that up with a couple of EP's which are just instrumentals like period piano music. I am working on a second full album and I'm excited about it because we are focusing on that vintage sound. You can find out more about this music at parlormuse.com.

Emz: Ed, Can you tell us a little bit about your film, *The Dead Matter?*

Ed: Before Midnight Syndicate, my first project right out of college was this movie called *The Dead Matter*. It's a movie about zombies and this amulet that can raise and control the dead and there are vampires involved. It's a nice little twisting and turning story. Back then though, we only had analog video tape and the quality of the image and audio was horrible. However, writing the score to the film did so much to start Midnight Syndicate. There were so many songs I wrote for the film that later became Midnight Syndicate songs. At any rate, many years later when we were scoring the film *The Rage* with Robert Kurtzman, I got to go on set and saw what a great production team he had in place. After *The Rage* wrapped, I asked him if he'd be interested in producing a remake of *The Dead Matter* with an actual budget. He liked the script and so we put together a group of investors, pulled his team together and filmed it. It's a fun movie, not quite as serious as Midnight Syndicate, but still nice and atmospheric. We shot on 16mm film so between that, the lighting, and the way we shot it, it's got that late-70s, early-80s horror look going. Most importantly though, I think it's an interesting story with plenty of twists and turns to keep you guessing. We've been really pleased with the response.

Emz: What are your favorite horror movies?

Gavin: For me, the original The Haunting *from 1963 is definitely my number one. It's black and white, all about subtly, just great ghost story, it gives a lot of room for your imagination to run. More recently,* The Conjuring *is a phenomenal film, the original* Halloween *from John Carpenter,* The Others, *there's been a lot of great things across the years.*

Ed: Watching horror films is my favorite hobby, so picking tops is kind of hard for me. Two of the movies that always seem to stay on top are *Night of the Living Dead* and *Evil Dead.* Seeing someone create something like that with a lower budget has always really inspired me as a filmmaker. *The Exorcist, Alien* and *Aliens, The Changeling,* anything Hammer Films released (including the new stuff!), *Old Dark House, The Ring, Sixth Sense, Haunted (1995), The Shining, Jaws* - there are so many and I love them all.

Emz: Do you have any favorite authors?

Ed: Stephen King, always has been. I love his work, I love his short story anthologies, he has definitely inspired more than a couple of songs.

Gavin: For me, Shirley Jackson was the writer for the Haunting of Hill House, *which was the basis for the movie* The Haunting, *so that's a classic. But also Algernon Blackwood wrote some really awesome ghost stories. Just atmospheric creepy stuff.*

Emz: What inspires you to create? How do you get into that creative space in your head?
Gavin: For me it's a lot of things. Movies, definitely. Other darker music, artwork. Draw the curtains, dim the lights, and get yourself into a place where a lot of those mysterious creep images start to inspire you.

Ed: Very similar for me as well. Horror films are definitely a big catalyst. When we're about to work on an album, I will immerse myself in horror movie marathons. I also find history is a great source of inspiration. When we did the *Carnival Arcane* album, researching actual carnivals from the turn of the century, finding out as much as we could about the environments we were trying to create, both musically and with sound effects was a really inspiring process. A classic Victorian or a scratchy black and white photo from the 19th century will kick my imagination into overdrive.

To find out more about Ed and Gavin, go to:
MidnightSyndicate.com

interview with valentine wolfe

by Dan Shaurette

Singer Sarah Black and bassist Braxton Ballew make up, Valentine Wolfe, a Victorian Chamber metal duo. That's right, I said "Victorian Chamber Metal". One of their albums used the phrase "Steampunk Macabre"—I like that, too. Braxton said, "We also perform Dark Ambient Soundscapes. Usually, if this is too vague, we tell people if they like Emilie Autumn and Nightwish, we like to think they will like us." Their song "Annabel Lee" from their album, *Once Upon a Midnight*, is themed around Edgar Allan Poe. Be still my little goth heart.

Braxton told me, "'Annabel Lee' is one of the songs off one of our recent releases. It is a graphic novel plus full length album all about Edgar Allan Poe. The graphic novel tells a story and the music follows along with it. The story puts Poe in an alternate universe where all of his stories and poems are his reality and so we set his work to go with that. Also, we feel it has all of the elements that make a Valentine Wolfe song: beautiful vocals, brooding classical bass, and slamming drums and distortion. The visual artist who did the cover of our last album, Jacob Wenzka, agreed to take a larger role this time around. He has drawn a graphic novel for our story about Poe. The album is not strictly programmatic, but it does follow a story in a very similar way to *Silverthorn* by Kamelot. I suppose the idea started when we saw a sketch Jacob had drawn of Poe. It was amazing! We thought we would like to see more. We had also been setting Shakespeare to music and that prompted us to think about how much fun it would be to set some of Poe's words to music. His poems are so lyrical anyway."

For the horror addicts who are *Deathstalker* fans, you may recognize the namesake of the band. Braxton confirmed that, "Valentine Wolfe is a character from the *Deathstalker* novels by Simon R. Green. He has somewhat of a depraved nature and we relate to that!"

More than just a duo, Sarah and Braxton are married and have been making music together since 2006. "We sometimes collaborate with other musicians and especially other artists, but we like to keep the main core as just a duo. We currently live in Greenville, SC. I would say that living in Greenville has certainly had a big impact on our music. Braxton works as the Education Director for the Greenville Symphony. That huge connection to the classical world has kept us from going in a fully metal direction. We have written music for three Shakespeare plays now: *The Merchant of Venice*, *Twelfth Night*, and *The Winter's Tale*. All of those were made possible by us living in a city that is so supportive of the arts. We have the Metropolitan Arts Council which really brings the whole community together through an impressive array of artistic endeavor."

With such an interesting style of music, the venues they have played are rather diverse. "We've played venues ranging from dive bars to art galleries. We really love playing fan conventions...it seems that's the best overall fit in terms of finding people who are interested in our music. I think it helps we're pretty geeky ourselves. We have played at several different conventions including RavenCon, AnachroCon, Upstate Steampunk, ConCarolinas, and DragonCon. We would love to play at Wave Gothic

Treffen or Whitby Gothic Weekend or even Wacken Open Air some day. Our fans are so amazing! They are willing to travel to see us perform in different cities and we really appreciate that. One thing we've seen at conventions, especially one where we're new, the crowd always seems to get bigger and bigger while we play. Just about every show is special-cliche, maybe, but true."

Braxton went on to say, "I think my favorite odd story was a show where I was doing solo bass soundscapes with looping. A gentleman asked me what instrument I was playing, and rejected my answer of electric upright bass to tell me it was, in fact, a cello (Hint-no, it isn't). I was still playing and looping the entire conversation, which made it even weirder."

Their favorite bands and musicians are as varied as one might expect: "Bach, Verdi, Handel, Mozart, Debussy, Ives, Copland, Beatles, Iron Maiden, Insomnium, Opeth, Nightwish, Kamelot, Amon Amarth, Dragonforce, Ronnie James Dio. Braxton's favorite bass player is an amazing player named Renaud Garcia-Fons. He's also really into Francois Rabbath."

Braxton summed up his musical tastes with a quote by Duke Ellington: "There's only two kinds of music: good and bad, and I like both." Braxton really only gets turned off to music that "seems to prioritize mass consumption to the exclusion of any other interesting features. But he thinks you can learn anything from anything (He listened to a Justin Bieber album for a group of kids, and was astounded at how the meaning of the song could be conveyed in only 3-5 seconds). We both think it's better not to spend too much time concerning yourself with what turns you off, and just focus on music that really excites you."

Is there a style of music that they'd like to try? Sarah said, "One style that we would like to explore more of is film scoring. We have written scores for plays so far and have done short movies for the internet, but we would love to do more! Braxton especially is a huge fan of what Philip Glass did for *Dracula* and we would love to do a film score for a feature length silent movie. We'd love to do an old one or a completely new one that is just in the style of an old one!"

Both have been making music for quite a while. "Sarah started on piano in elementary school and kept up with that up through college. She got a Bachelor and Master's degree in Composition from UGA. She has been taking voice lessons with Lisa Barksdale most recently. Braxton is a late bloomer-bass guitar at age 14, double bass at age 18, composition at 20 (apart from a few aborted attempts in high school). However, he's kind of old-he's been at this for about 20 years as a pro."

What is it like to produce music? "It's always exhilarating and terrifying. You get an idea that sets your passion on fire, and it becomes an obsession. At the same time, you hope and want your peers and your audience to get into what you're doing. The hardest part is waiting. Works of quality take time. Sometimes, you want to just work and work and work, and the hardest part is knowing when you pass the point of diminished returns. The most fun part has been playing the new songs live, and seeing the savage joy they trigger."

How has producing their latest album been different than their previous work? "There are two basic differences: we blended the composition/performance approach. Generally, in the classical world, you write a piece, sending it out into the world more or less fully formed, and then you learn and interpret the piece through rehearsals and performances. Sometimes you get to revise in a rehearsal, but not often. This time, we played everything we wrote either live or in the rehearsal studio several times through. It enabled us to add small and significant touches to everything. On our first two albums, we wanted to explore EBM and electronica. As such, there's synth basses and other electronica textures we play with. For *Once Upon A Midnight*, we fully embraced our inner metalhead. There's still electronica, but almost all limited to double bass (there's a bit of piano here and there). So while we're still very much a band who loves electronica, I'd say this album is definitely gothic metal."

Music is so much a part of their life, working together as a couple and a band, there's little time for diversions. Sarah said, "Not working with the band? We didn't even realize that was an option! We are a married couple and we spend just about every waking second involved with some aspect of music making. It is nice for us because we both have the same passion and drive to immerse ourselves in a non-stop musical adventure. We do also enjoy reading and movies. That is where much of our inspiration comes from. I'm into video games, too. I really have ambitions to make a silent movie one of these days."

So, what is next on their radar? "We need to finish up the recording and mixing on this current project but after that, we'd love to travel around for more shows. We played at several conventions last year, but we want to try to get to twice as many this year! So we have some great new music that we are finishing up and the next step will be sharing that new music with as many people as we can reach."

They have some great, practical advice for new bands. "Watch the Ira Glass video on the gap between taste and execution as much as you can. If you want to make this your main source of income, limit your debt as much as practical. Follow your own instincts as a fan. In other words, what kinds of shows do you like going to? What kinds of sounds, experiences, etc, do you value; that is, more importantly than even money: where do you invest your time? If you can get a clear answer to those type of questions, you can get a pretty accurate road map of your trajectory. Oddly, don't obsess too much about being 'good'. Everyone defines that differently. As long as the best show you play is your next one, that's a pretty good way to think about it."

Top 10 Horror Soundtracks
by HorrorAddicts.net

1. *Suspiria*
2. *Lost Boys*
3. *Dracula*
4. *Interview with the Vampire*
5. *Sweeny Todd*
6. *Beetlejuice*
7. *Nightmare Before Christmas*
8. *The Crow*
9. *Scream*
10. *Queen of the Damned*

Zombie Night

by Emerian Rich

New horror lyrics to be sung to the tune of:
"O Holy Night" originally composed by Adolphe Adam to the
poem by Placide Cappeau.

Oh, Zombie Night. The world is for your taking.
It is the night when your hunger will reign.
Long lay the world in peace and Zed-free slumber
Till you appear and then all hell breaks loose
A shrill, a scream, and all the children frightened.
A father clutches shotgun to his breast.

Fall on your knees
Pretend the terror's over.
Oh, Zombie Night.
Oh, psyche. You rise again.
Oh, Zombie Night.
Oh, Zombie... You rise again.

Town leads a band to fight and to destroy you.
You aren't the kind that goes down without a bite.
Here come the guns, the torches, and the rednecks
But you have one more trick up your bloody sleeve.
Cousin Bob, ya see, he has become one
And they are screwed cause he is in their ranks.

Feast on their Flesh (Bob)
Oh, feast and share a plenty.
Oh, Zombie Night.
Oh, psyche. Bob rises again.
Oh, Zombie Night.
Oh, Zombie... You rise again.

Sun in the East is calling for the morning
And zombies rest in a peaceful, glutton sleep.
Timmy is hiding way up in church rafters,
He's got a gun and he'll burn you zombies down.
One thing he has never even thought of
Is mother's face looking up from down below.

Mom is undead.
Timmy can't kill his mommy.
Oh, Zombie Night.
Oh, psyche. Mom rises again.
Oh, Zombie Night.
Oh, Zombies... We rise again.

HORROR ART

nightshade on art

Hello again my addicts, in this section we talk about art. It's not hard to find good horror art out there. You can Google "horror art" and you will be able to find lots of different horror artists. They all have different ideas on what's scary, and looking at their work, you get to put a picture to the things that scare you the most. Some horror art is even popular in the mainstream. Two of my favorites are "The Nightmare" by Henry Fuseli and "The Scream" by Edvard Munch.

I always wondered, what is the guy in "The Scream" screaming about? Is there a zombie after him? Did a serial killer say he was going to kill him? Or maybe his underwear is on too tight. Of course, in reality he is probably a horror addict like us and he is screaming because he can't understand why there are people out there who don't understand it. Or at least that's my story and I'm sticking to it.

Whether you like classics like Munch and Dali, or the more modern HR Giger or Victoria Frances, I think you have to agree that horror art must do one thing, and that is: invoke a feeling of fear or dread (even if it's a pleasant dread) upon the observer.

My art can invoke fear all right, but not the right kind. I always wonder why my stick figures didn't quite make the grade. Could it be the daggers they hold or the blood pooling at their feet?

easy horror doodles

by Emerian Rich

SPIDERWEB

BAT

PUMPKIN

SPIDER

Cover Artist
Masloski Carmen

by Emerian Rich

Cover artist for *Horror Addicts Guide to Life*, Masloski Carmen, lives in Romania. Her parents taught her how to respect and value things, and gave her the freedom to choose her own path.

I discovered Masloski's work when I was looking for a cover for our first anthology, *The Wickeds*, on DeviantArt.com. I was beginning to lose hope. I couldn't find anything that conveyed the dark beauty we wanted for *The Wickeds*. Just as I was about to give up, I found Masloski's *Silent Wind* which spoke to me in a way I can't explain. Although *Silent Wind* was a great piece of artwork, I wanted to incorporate our witchy feel and Masloski was awesome to work with. She came up with a glowing green orb to place in the model's hands and I knew as soon as I saw it, that was the cover for us.

For this book, Masloski created a new piece of art using the elements our editor, David Watson, wanted to be included. He asked for a monster school setting with a chalkboard, and the cover of this book shows what Masloski came up with.

Now, you get to find out a little more about Masloski, her art, and what kind of art she enjoys.

Emerian: What is your favorite thing about your country?
Masloski: I really enjoy some parts of Romanian Folklore. I like some regional music, ancient winter games, clothes, legends/stories/myths, and dances.

Emerian: What was your childhood like?
Masloski: I was one of those kids full of energy, spending their entire time playing outside and drawing when bored.

Emerian: How did you know you wanted to be an artist?
Masloski: When I drew on my parents' furniture. The drawings are still there!

Emerian: What is your earliest memory of art that touched you?
Masloski: It wasn't a specific piece. I was really impressed by some people's ability to draw things so perfectly, fast, and beautiful.

Emerian: What inspires you to create?
Masloski: Critical situations and stressful moments. Of course, there's always my music, old engravings, baroque and rococo times, myths, psychological movies like mind-twisters, circus elements, and the contrast between things (ie: horror-cute, cold-hot, dark-bright and so on).

Emerian: What is your favorite thing to draw?
Masloski: Mixed things mostly. Animals with human bodies, dolls, hybrids, religion-themes, circus themes, and musical elements.

Emerian: What is your favorite piece of art that you have done?
Masloski: *Symphony of Death*

Emerian: How did you get involved in the working with HorrorAddicts.net?
Masloski: I was really lucky that you found me on DeviantArt.com and asked me to collaborate with *The Wickeds*.

Emerian: What is your favorite time of day?
Masloski: Between 1–4 a.m. I get my ideas in that time of the day and I even work during those hours.

Emerian: What are your favorite books to read?
Masloski: Short horror stories (something similar with creepy-pasta stories), history, and psychological books.

Emerian: Do you have a favorite artist or piece of artwork?
Masloski: I have some favorite artists like Francisco Goya, Zdzislaw Beksinski, Paul Kuczynsky, (one of my best resources and inspirational artist), and Jenny Marie ("Autonoe" from DeviantArt).

Emerian: Where can the readers find out more about you?
Masloski: People can find me at:
http://mskycarmen.deviantart.com

Top 10 Horror Artists
by Emerian Rich

1. Edward Gorey
2. HR Giger
3. Victoria Frances
4. Gerald Brom
5. Salvador Dali
6. Kaori Yuki
7. Cliff Nielsen
8. Dave McKean
9. Nene Thomas
10. Chris Kuchta

interview with bill Rude

by David Watson

For you horror art lovers out there, here is an interview with Bill Rude. There are a lot of great horror artists out there, but Bill is one of our favorites.

When did you start drawing?

Probably like most people, I've been drawing since I was a little kid. High school helped me focus my interest in pursuing art and helped me land a scholarship to the Minneapolis College of Art + Design. The twist here was that I was a film major and all my classes were film and photography! The drawing I did in art school was mostly on my own time when I would draw pictures depicting the Dungeons and Dragons games my friends and I would play.

Who inspired you to start drawing?

That's a big question. In the real world, mostly my parents. They really reinforced the idea that pursuing creative work was something that could become a reality. In the 'art' world, it was a lot of fantasy and horror illustrators. Frank Frazetta, Bernie Wrightson, Larry Elmore.... and let's not forget Derek Riggs and all his Iron Maiden album covers!

What is the best and worst thing about being a horror artist?

I believe any successful artist is one who is simply creating whatever they want to create, regardless of popularity or profit. That being said, the best thing about being a horror artist is that it is not just a genre, but a community of people who have a built-in interest in the subject matter. There is a level of support in the horror community that truly facilitates being able to do whatever I want in the genre, because it just so happens to jive with what people are interested in seeing.

The worst thing about being a horror artist is the unavoidable envy of so many other artists that rock the genre. So many different styles. So many different takes. So inspirational and so intimidating at the same time.

How long does it take for you to finish a project?

It really depends on the project, but it can range anywhere from just a few hours to maybe a full week of non-stop work. If I'm creating one of my fake movie posters or pulp novel covers, the painting normally takes about three days. Then probably another two or three days to layout the design work. Those particular pieces are all created as 24×36 shadowboxes, where the design work is printed directly onto acrylic glass and floated over the top of the original painting. That will then take another week or two to have that stuff fabricated and put together. Of course that's a part of the process I have done by other people, but it still contributes to the time line I've got to consider if I'm creating something for a show or commission. Then none of this takes into account the research! Before I start any project there is usually a minimum full-day of researching the subject matter and figuring out styles and concepts.

What inspires you the most when you take on a project?

There are probably two facets to my inspiration. First is trying to depict the concept of character. At my core I'm a story-teller, so when I create something visual, it is intended to depict the subject matter in a very particular way. Could be the expression on the face of a monster, or freezing a particular moment of action. Bottom line though, is that there is always a character implying motivation, whether they be good or bad.

The second facet is the actual process. For example, If I'm inspired to do another illustration in my fairy tale series, a lot of it has to do with me wanting to recreate some texture with only pen and ink—like 'Little Miss Muffet' has shiny, glassy eyes on the spider with coarse hair on its legs, and a clean beautiful face on Miss Muffet herself. Another example is in a piece I recently did for a tribute show to the film *The Iron Giant*. It's one of my favorite movies of all time, and I knew I could identify the scariest scene in the movie to jive with my horror work, but it wasn't until I became interested in working with only black and white ink washes to create ocean waves in a hurricane that I committed to the show. I'd only done one other ink wash drawing before, and never worked with white ink, so that is what drew me in.

What makes you want to make horrific art?

To me the worlds of horror represent outsiders. In the same way that Goth culture embraces dark themes as an appealing concept, I want to weave together worlds where scary situations are commonplace, but they are also beautiful, inspirational, or funny. If I'm able to connect with a viewer on that additional, emotionally positive hook, then they know this is actually a welcoming place for an outsider exactly like themselves. The nightmares I create are intended to be friendly, but it may take the right kind of person to recognize that.

What is your concept of horror?
At the root I believe horror to be anything unfamiliar that exists with confidence. It is intended to be a relatively broad definition that I can fit all of my different series of work under, but really the only thing that changes from theme to theme is the perspective of who finds it horrifying. The idea that the monster from the lab is walking through town, trying to find help, is horrifying to the peasants. Tiki idols of long forgotten gods still standing on the volcano slopes of a deserted island are horrifying to the western explorers. A beautiful woman confidently wearing a bikini is horrifying to Puritans. Using that sliding scale, it's then easy to apply to real world outsiders like goths, burlesque dancers, teenagers racing cars… from someone's perspective all of those things are horrifying, and mostly because they are unfamiliar.

Why do you like to make art that has a retro or nostalgic feel to it?
I'm a rockabilly boy at heart, and have always been obsessed with the concept of nostalgia and the perception of historical life. At the time, no one creating low-budget monster movies or magazine art thought of it as anything more than contemporary culture. But when we look back at it now, we are only using hind-sight, and what only really represented four or five years of a certain cultural style is perceived to be its own separate world that lasted

decades and never evolved into anything else stylistically.

For that reason, I want to essentially weave a world where that culture is still going on. It's intended to start at a baseline of an idealized past, and then draw people's personal experiences into it. An example of a piece of mine that is well received in that fashion is "Fright 36". It's a large print, on very expensive paper, and replicates an advertisement page (page 36) from a 1960s horror magazine that never existed (*Fright Magazine*). It's the standard collection of creepy t-shirts and mail order gags. But when some people see it, blown up and framed, hanging in a gallery, a flood of memories and stories come back to them as kids. They remember the mystery of just what the hell were you going to actually get if your parents let you order something from that magazine? And it only really works because it is implied to be of that time, and you're forcing them to look through that nostalgic lens that is emotionally enhancing what they are looking at.

Of course nostalgia and authenticity is only the polish on the world I'm creating. In the example of "Fright 36", that print actually ties other work of mine together. Connecting to some fake pulp novel covers I've painted, which then connect to more. Then across the top of the "Fright" print is an ad for "Horrifying Monster T-Shirts", one of which I have had made as a real T-shirt and make for sale. And on the hang tag of the physical shirt is a made up history of that T-shirt design and why they aren't around anymore. When people connect those dots and see all of that work in one place, the reaction can be incredible. I've literally had people have to recompose themselves before leaving my booth at a trade show. Grown men, with just a look, will be like, "You did it.

You actually created the world we all wanted to be real when we were kids."

What are some of the other projects you worked on?

A couple of years ago my buddy Chris 'Doc' Wyatt and myself, developed an animated TV show that was turned into a Graphic Novel, called *Creepsville*, and was essentially a horror version of *Futurama*. Four high school kids, each an outcast for different reasons, are forced to work on the school newspaper together. It turns out that their high school is in a town, in a world, where all B-Movies are real. The outcasts are a cow girl, a zombie, a child genius, and an amphibious foreign exchange student.

I'm also currently working on a couple of art-books, one of which is a coffee table book of horrific Christmas legends from around the world. The second is an expanded collection of my fake b-movie poster paintings in the guise of a fake 1960s Horror magazine, called *Fright*.

My day job is working in the film industry as a designer and animator. That brings a lot of crossover with horror and general retro design. Everything from doing on-set special effects on *Ghost Whisperer* to designing T-shirts for characters on *True Blood*. Lots of low-budget horror and sci-fi projects. And of course I designed and animated the titles for the last four *American Girl* movies, based off of the dolls. This is a true story.

How did you get involved in dressing up as Krampus?

One of my series of work are classically drawn fairy tale illustrations. All horrific, of course. Depicting the most frightening moments in stories like "Little Red

Riding Hood" or "Hansel and Gretel." As a part of that, I did an illustration of Krampus, the Alpine Christmas Demon and created holiday cards for the season. One day I was delivering an order of cards to Meltdown Comics, in Hollywood, and we were like, "Wouldn't it be great if someone would appear as Krampus around the holidays so people didn't have to take their kids for photos with Santa at the mall every year?." Cut to two weeks later and I had put together a costume and had appearances booked all over the area.

That was about three years ago. Now it's essentially a full-time job around the holidays. There is now a Los Angeles Krampus Troupe I'm also a part of, but they are pretty legit and organize their own events and are really good at keeping the authenticity of the Austrian Krampus traditions alive. I'm sort of recognized as LA's original Krampus who does the whole Mickey Mouse thing to move merchandise.

What do you like about Krampus?

To me Krampus is that necessary naughty side to the nice that is promoted through the holidays. Traditionally, Krampus is never without St. Nicholas, so it was never intended to be an overwhelmingly dark and scary addition to the holiday. Sure, the Austrian Krampus runs can get pretty intense, but St. Nick is leading it all and people are having fun.

What I like about Krampus, which reflects on how I portray him, is that he represents an opportunity for people to confront their fears. For kids they are confronting the monster under the bed. Krampus is only going to warn them not to be naughty, and they will have nothing to fear. Krampus is about not being scared.

My Krampus appearances are almost always public in nature, with a lot of strangers just stumbling upon me being there, and it is remarkable how kids really are not afraid of Krampus. When it comes down to it, kids are only afraid of what their parents tell them to be afraid of. People may have various reasons not to let their kids participate in a Krampus appearance, but when they say, "Oh, no, my kids would be too scared to visit Krampus." I only hear the words "Because I'm a disconnected parent who does not have a responsible relationship with my children." Parents: be responsible. Let your kids get a free photo with Krampus.

Did you make the Krampus suit yourself?

I assembled the Krampus costume myself, but didn't actually make anything. Everything is off the shelf, but I do feel there is a level of originality and character I breathe into it by how I put the various elements together and portray him. A lot of thought was put into incorporating the giant basket on my back, and the few fabric/clothing elements of the costume. It also helps that in costume, my Krampus comes out to almost 7 feet tall. You want a character whose mere presence can fill a room.

For more information on Bill Rude check out:
7hells.com

Giger memorial

by Mimielle

Maybe this was your first contact. 1979, when the word 'alien' was truly redefined forever. Or perhaps like myself, you're older, and were more shocked at a younger age when the bizarrely beautiful works of HR Giger were a bit newer.

No matter when you first saw Giger's work, I am sure it was a memorable moment, a questioning and perhaps eerie moment. Yes? Yes!

Then you are more like me than I even imagined. I have tried to write an obituary for HR Giger, but it more becomes a reflection, like his work. He was a private man, eschewing the spotlight in the dawning age of celebrity and in a time when illustration, design and fine art were perceived as more separate. He preferred to let his work speak for him. I respect that and have always looked to his art and never his fame or personal details. The hard and precise yet moody airbrush, the organic yet metal shapes, the reflection of us all that he captured when we weren't looking. These things are what speak to me and that is both the beauty and the horror that is his art. It is compelling. Unforgettable.

Alien's co-writer, Dan O'Bannon, recalled meeting Giger for the first time, in a Paris hotel. Giger offered him some opium. O'Bannon asked why he took it. "I am afraid of my visions," Giger replied. "It's just your mind," O'Bannon said. Giger responded, "That is what I am afraid of."*

I may never get to see a Giger Bar but at least my avatar in Second Life has a reproduction of one of the chairs. In my Second Life living room, my own art hangs on the wall, the segmented and quasi-organic shapes clearly inspired by Giger's works. His influence reached far and will never stop reaching and growing. Better than any obituary, it is a testament to the meeting of minds and the questions he asked. Of himself, of us all, and now of the universe itself. HR Giger, 1940-2014

In a New York Times obituary, Timothy Leary, a friend of Giger's, was quoted as having praised the artist by saying, "Giger's work disturbs us, spooks us, because of its enormous evolutionary time span. It shows us, all too clearly, where we come from and where we are going."*

None of us knows when we will go, or to where. Visions from HR Giger will continue to both haunt my nightmares as well as inspire.

Stay Beautiful, addicts! ~Mimielle

Sources & Credits: New York Times, The Guardian, Giger Museum, Omni Magazine, Damianos Giger Chair in Second Life.

HORROR WRITING

niGhtShade on wRiting

Horror writers are a special group of people. You might not think it, but most horror writers are the nicest people you would ever want to meet. I think it's because they get all their fears out in their writing and it's a form of release. Who needs a psychiatrist when you can just write down what scares you?

Everyone should aspire to be a horror writer. You can write someone you don't like into a horror story and have a vampire or killer massacre him in the worst possible way. If you ask me, that's great therapy. Writing is like creating a world and then being in charge of what happens there.

Some people might think writing horror is easy. Just build a world, add a monster, and then axe a few people. But this art form takes a little more imagination than that. After all, who wants to kill someone the way everyone else does it? Adding a little variety in your torture scenes takes some time, a large cup of whatever your poison is, and some real-life know-how.

I write horror a little differently, it's more like an instruction manual for me. I write about how I'm going to torture my enemies and then try to see if I can reenact the death scene exactly as I wrote it. I sure hope my victims appreciate my artistry.

being a horror editor

by Eden Royce

Even with a strong comprehension of grammar, spelling and punctuation, editing isn't an easy job. I've edited for years, meticulously adding every missed comma (deleting some extra ones) and pairing lonely quotation marks with their mates. This simple copy editing has its trials but it's *nothing* like being a submissions editor. Especially a Horror Submissions Editor. (Picture that title in a creepy Hammer Horror movie font. It deserves it.)

The job of submissions editor isn't akin to getting licked by kittens. Your task is to read massive amounts of slush—stories submitted to a press for consideration—and decide what will be published and what won't. If you're lucky, you have a team of slush readers to go through all of the completely unacceptable stories submitted. I now have slushies (Mmm…slushies), but when I started it was all me: writing the submission call, reading the stories, and sending the decisions. (Well, me and a glass of saké.)

Sometimes you get what you asked for in the call for submissions and the sun comes out and rainbows cover the land. Or rather, darkness clouds your world and wraps you tightly in a cocoon of fascinated disturbia from which you want no escape. Other times, not so much. In one instance, I edited a horror anthology and the call requested frightening horror tales—no vampires or werewolves, though—and I received a story about a boy with uncontrollable diarrhea. The author's cover email stated that he could not think of anything more terrifying. *Blink, blink*

Like most editors, my main piece of advice to authors is to read what the press is looking for and try to submit the best work that you (really, truly in your heart of hearts) think fits.

Great segue into the next thing: you must have a sense of humor or else you'll go insane. Despite the resurgence of interest in Lovecraft's work, that's not a place I'd like to go. As much as I try to answer questions about or describe what it is the press wants to see, there is an unknown that's impossible to quantify. A certain intangible something—the clichéd *je ne sais quoi*—that can't be put into words. Authors have expressed frustration with this, but it can't be helped. While an editor can't tell you ahead of time what would make a powerful and evocative story, he or she knows immediately when one turns up in the reading list. It's the feeling you get when drawn completely into a book, especially one that you didn't count on grabbing your interest. After the final word, you sit in your comfy chair for a moment and look at the text again, wanting more to appear. Then you shake your head as if clearing the last remnants of the tale from your mind. But it's futile. Part of that story will always be with you. You know it's one worth sharing. You want to tell someone about it. And that's when an editor sends an acceptance.

Editing is hard work, but finding jewels of stories and presenting them to readers is worth the work. They're presented, of course, after hours of handling contracts, rewrites, continuity checks, proofreading, formatting, working with artists on cover design…. *Sigh* It's enough to drive a person mad.

But it's worth embracing the madness.

WRITING EXTREME HORROR

by Catt Dahman

I am all over the horror writing scene as a writer, an editor, opinion-giver, and more. I watch trends and try to predict them, but at no time have there ever been so many variables. Some may feel we are zombie/vamp swamped, but while those are still favorite topics, there are more sub-genres than ever before. It reminds me of the 60s-70s influx of new horror.

There is some badly written material, I agree, but there is just as much badly written horror from those who are with huge presses as those who self-publish. I don't see the difference, except for the ones who are getting paid enormous sums for shlock. I also don't want to talk about the B-horror/ commercial writing (that many of us have done to support the other writing we wish to do). It has a place if we trust in *Sharknado 2* (it is entertaining and I still indulge), but I want to talk about the rest.

I had to get the rest off my plate to get here, to the trends I am seeing in horror that are interesting. One is the splatter-punk/ splatter-gore/ extreme horror genre. I like it. I describe it in a book's forward as not shooting tequila, but snorting it. Occasionally, it's fun to read those types. I prefer them, actually. Why? Again, some are bad, some are B-list, and so on, but I like those that are spot-on, well written, and brutal. They get a bad reputation because they often contain explicit sex (and sex is so bad, right?), and because they have gore, and because of the unconventional, profane themes.

That is the real kicker. The other elements, we can set aside, and maybe complain about, but the themes are what bother us. Extreme horror magnifies the themes. I love the subtlety of *The Lottery* or in *Frankenstein*; I get the social and personal over tones, but sometimes… There are times I want to snort the tequila.

Some of the extreme horror stories I have read recently are raunchy, profane, and rough. They are also very honest, and they hit some disturbing themes harder than the more subtle pieces can. One, recently, blew me away. *Pubienne Tueur de Cheveux* by Scott Pratt has given me nightmares. It reads as a piece that contains sex, language, and a mature theme. It seems just a simple, extreme piece, and all would be fine if that were the end. Instead, it bothered me deeply as a social piece of writing. Within, hidden very well, are some ideas that are disturbing.

Pratt discusses a woman's place, treatment of sexual abuse victims, legal politics, sexual preferences, and the difference in power/strength/bitchery that some face. The story may be wrapped in a nice package of sexual overtones, gore, and offensive (but honest and real) action, but the real horror is within the very theme.

I am fascinated with these types of stories. How clever is it that the writers hide deep commentary within the fancy gift-wrapping? The stories are so honest and they cut so deeply, that they simply must be hidden within a special means of dispersal. What else but the horror genre can cover the deeper meanings? To me, that is a new trend of horror that I am in love with. I am enjoying reading the stories, but have mixed feelings.

Several other presses have rejected these that I have been pouring over. Why? Oh, the themes mainly, of course, because they are shocking. If the acquisitions editor who read them was not a deep-thinker, then the stories were tossed back for the content (sex, gore, language). I get amused. I get scared. That is, I get amused and scared when I read the stories and when I consider the fact that I am going to release them.

I am a writer of commercial horror (read B-shlock), thrillers, zombies, and some more classic type, literary horror. I have one or two extreme books as well. Of 35+ books, I have found the shlock and the extreme sell the best. That was kind of what got me here, to being the editor who might release stories that no other press will touch. Why do those of mine sell the best? What is the trend?

Honesty.

In my commercial works and in the extreme, I am free to be as honest and brutal as I please. I can hit home the ideas we don't want to always think about: abuse, intolerance, bad parenting, and my favorite: bad family traditions. I get to say what I feel, but wrap it up in a pretty package of gore and violence, and hide my social commentary. I hide the honesty within the sex. I put the real fear behind the shadows of some foul language. In this way, I can deliver my story, nicely tucked into something that seems like fun, but is in no way light. Does this make sense? I hide the real fear and horror behind a story of pretend horror that is overdone and extreme. And guess what? It sells and people love those pieces the most.

Some don't get it. A few rant and rave and call me on the fake horror. That makes me laugh. They don't get it. A few do get it, and they love what I have said. They are also scared by both the real and the fake. That's when I have hit it out of the ole ball park, when I get them and then they get the message behind the horror.

I get it. I really get it. So when I read one of these schlocky, profane, or bizarre stories, I know what the author is truly saying. I get the real message of sheer terror that is hidden in gossamer layers and tied with silken bows. Those stories really scare me. They really are, at times, like snorting tequila. They hurt.

I like the trend, but not everyone does or will. It's way too much for some. Unfortunately, some very smart readers will refuse to read this type of story when the pieces are secretly written for the most intelligent of readers. The smart readers sometimes don't see that the stories are written for *them*. It's a subgenre that kicks those that it is aimed at, but isn't that the idea? Kick and hit? Gut-punch and eviscerate?

Horror will always be fun and have the B-list, commercial fun stuff. It will always deliver the books that are excellent, classic and literary, but there is room for a new sub-genre. There is a place for the intelligently profane. It may take a while to be recognized for brilliancy, but it's strong in a (fitting, very apt) hidden subculture of writers and readers. It's the Jimi Hendrix, the Kurt Cobain, Elvis, Jim Morrison and the Janis Joplin of the literary world. They were once considered "dangerous to the youth" and only admired by a few. Today, they are viewed as revolutionary. Motown was once thought to be a bad influence. None of those musical giants harmed music, they changed it for the better.

I feel the intellectual profane horror will do the same. It will take a while, but in time, names we may not know now (Goforth, Misura, Fisher, Johnson, Woods, Keane, Pratt, and more) will be whispered about. They will be called revolutionary or so emulated that they may be forgotten, but I am thrilled to say I was there. No, I didn't get to see Hendrix play live at Woodstock, but I am getting to see a few as they begin the revolution, and to me, brother, that is big time.

Horror is a'changin'.

And the best part, is, I get it. And I am there this time.

Rattling Bones and Writing Horror

by Chris Ringler

Oh, pity us poor fools who fall in love with the horror genre. Pity us because once you're in love, man, it's hard to kick the old ghost outta bed in the morning. I, for better or worse, love horror and part of that love came from the movies and writers I found as a kid. The logical outcome of this silly infatuation with horror was to jump knee deep into it, which I did. Now, I am a writer of no great import or fame. I have had my nods toward legitimacy, but those aren't the reasons I write. No. I write because I have to. And I think that's the heck of it with anyone that works in the arts. You do it because you have no choice.

I started pretty simply, writing stories high on blood and imitation and low on real chills, but these old stories were the first steps I took as a writer, and without those old stories, I wouldn't be where I am today. Now, I didn't set out to be a horror writer, and am not sure I would say I am wholly one now. I can tell you that I write stories meant to remind you of what it was like to be a child in the dark, when all is quiet but for the sounds coming from your closet or under your bed or deep within the shadows. I started writing, seriously writing, because of all the weirdness roaming around in me, the germs of stories waiting to be born. It was like wherever I was, whatever I was doing, I could see some potential for horror. Now, I have never had aspirations to be the next big anyone, nor have I tried to imitate any of the people that influenced me, but it's hard not to want to honor the writers that filled you with the passion in the first place.

And that's where you get to the core of it. I write for a couple reasons—the passion and the past. I write because I have to. Even when it aggravates me, when it drives me nuts, when it makes me wonder why on earth I keep doing it, well, even then I keep writing, even when the fear of never getting anything seen creeps in you still keep writing. It's a passion that drives you. A fire that can't be put out, no matter what you do. And after the passion, there's the past. The want and desire to pay forward the things that influenced you. The want to inspire people as you were inspired and thus get people to look at the people who inspired you. As a writer, I have so many people that inspired me I feel I owe some debt to them for their work and their inspiration. So, I want to write stories as a tribute, in the hopes I can capture some of the darkness they passed to me. We pass this darkness from person to person to person in the hope of keeping intelligent, scary, good horror alive.

Writing is a challenge, but it's always been a challenge and always will be. The challenge now comes in getting it out there. The publishers are not taking as many looks at new fiction as they used to, and the same goes for agents and magazines. So it hasn't gotten easier. Only, it has. With self-publishing starting to gain legitimacy and the advent of the internet, you can always have an avenue to get your work out. Patience is always the key when it comes to writing. It's a process. A mantra—write, edit, write, edit, edit, edit, and edit some more. It's daunting but is worthwhile. It is amazing, really. With the advent of e-Books and e-Readers, we have a new world opening up to us. Me, I dream of a day when I can match a story with images, video, footnotes, every manner of device that will not bog the story down, but which will help tell it, to advance it. It's scary…and so exciting to think of what technology will do for the story. It sometimes seems as if books and reading are passing away but they aren't, they are simply evolving and we're at the edge of that evolution. We are creating that evolution with all we are doing. It's our job now, not just to tell good stories, but to figure out how to make technology help us tell our stories in new and exciting ways. We need to learn to tell our stories in ways that will make them live past today, past tomorrow, and will inspire those that come after us to keep scaring another and to keep books and writing alive. And as for me, I'll be waiting for you, not under your bed, or in your closet, but just out of sight and watching from the dark, and waiting, quietly. Waiting for you to just fall asleep.

how to become an immortalized author (like poe)

by Garth von Buchholz

One could argue successfully that gothic icon Edgar Allan Poe not only achieved more fame after his death in 1849 at a withered 40 years of age, but that in the 21st century he has become more celebrated and more of a brand name than many of the most lofty writers of his century. Ask a random person on the street if they've heard of Byron, Emerson, Hawthorne, Keats, Shelley, Tennyson, Wordsworth, and you'll likely elicit a blank stare unless they are students of 19th century literature, but utter the name "Poe" and you'll have said enough to be rewarded with a smile and nod of recognition. They might even cite "The Raven" or "The Tell-tale Heart" as a work they've read (or seen in the movies—it hasn't harmed Poe's reputation that filmmakers in the last century have cinematized stories from his feverish imagination.)

If you are a writer who hasn't yet achieved Poe's level of success in life, then consider these words a balm of Gilead because there is still hope for your literary reputation *post mortem*. That undeserved rejection slip, that unpublished 800-page masterpiece, that undelivered public reading of your most cryptic poetry cycle—all will be redeemed someday after your bones have found their resting place, whether in an oven or in soil, provided you carefully consider and slavishly follow these diabolically clever tips for becoming an Immortalized Author.

1. Alienate any family members with money who might share it with you someday. Poe managed to alienate his foster father, John Allan. His haughty attitude and behaviour towards the surly merchant only thickened the man's resolve not to adopt Poe or leave him any kind of financial legacy. Ironic that Poe is best known today as Edgar Allan Poe when he always signed his name with only the initial "A" throughout his lifetime: Edgar A. Poe. Even that's ironic that he would continue to use the initial that stood for the name of the man who rejected him so completely. Although this was only one cause of Poe's poverty, it started a chain reaction of pennilessness for many years forward. **Remember:** If you have any extended relatives who might gift you with money or property, be certain to drive them away forever with your arrogance, dismissive words and plain loathing. Poverty is your best friend if you want to live the romantic life of the threadbare artist.

2. Alienate writers, reviewers, editors, publishers, patrons and anyone else whose sphere of influence and good name might help promote your writing. Poe never learned you can be an author, you can be a reviewer, but you can't be an author and a reviewer. Believe me, I've been a creator and a critic at the same time and it doesn't work. Try socializing with authors whose books you've trashed. Or try the same with critics who have savaged your precious work. Poe was a master critic, but it also made him widely despised by writers and editors alike. Even the few friends or allies he had in literary circles eventually turned their backs on him because of his untamed, undiscriminating tongue that lashed out at them as cruelly as he did to his enemies. **Remember:** Become a literary critic and try your damndest to destroy the artistic reputations of other writers so nary an author in the world will ever desire to say anything in your favour ever again. *The only exception to this rule is #3 below.*

3. Practice a seductive form of sycophancy by praising to the heavens the works of women (or men) you lust after. While Poe alienated male writers who admired his work and sought to befriend him, he was always keen on lauding the mediocre or even substandard literary output of women he desired. It might have also been a ploy to make them dependent on him alone for their self-esteem for it was hard indeed for a woman in Poe's era to break into the old boys' club of literature. Imagine what the male writers of his time, including the ones he annihilated with his pen, thought of his support of the largely untalented Frances Sargent Osgood. **Remember:** Always be willing to sacrifice your own integrity as an artist if you can be rewarded with the attentions of those of lesser ability, regardless of whether they are married or not.

4. Drink alcohol frequently. Copious amounts of alcohol. No doubt many contemporary writers reading this advice may already be highly efficient in this tactic, and may in fact have more expertise on the matter than I do. Poe, however, was the ultimate "cheap drunk" who even admitted in writing that it took only a sip of the devil's nectar for him to descend into debauchery and shame. In an age where men only drank with other men, carried flasks of booze in their hip pockets, and caroused with drink in the streets and at work, Poe still managed to attain notoriety as a boss alcoholic who shocked his tippling and non-tippling peers alike. Drinking may have also directly or indirectly led to his death when he was found dying in a gutter, seemingly inebriated but more likely having suffered some physical indignities after a recent binge. **Remember:** Self-abuse through alcohol can effectively age you prematurely and speed the undertaker to your doorstep. It can also lead to wild mood swings, erratic and violent behaviour, social disgrace, and other dire consequences such as loss of work (see #5 below) which will naturally help to immortalize you as well. It seemed to work for Charles Bukowski, too.

5. Skillfully avoid anything resembling a regular job with a paycheque. In point #1, I illustrated the importance of living in poverty if you wish to become a legend after death. And in point #4 I mentioned how well alcoholism can limit your ability to sustain employment, but Poe was not only skillful at losing paying jobs as an editor through his drinking, but also at finding ways to avoid any kind of career opportunity that might lift him from his pauper's misery. Once he almost managed to land a plum clerical job in government by begging a favour from a friend in the civil service. Other authors such as Johann von Goethe made a solid living in the civil service, and a government job would have rescued Poe, his wife Virginia, and his Aunt Maria Clemm from starvation and other hardships. So what did Poe do? He went on a bender the night before his interview and missed the interview, as if he feared success or simply didn't want to have to hold a responsible job. **Remember:** Writing is your only job, and avoiding gainful employment is the only way you'll have sufficient time to nurture your writer's block without interruption.

6. Finally, write as little as you can when you do have time to write, and write amusing essays

such as this one instead of following your literary muse. Given that Poe spent most of his life not working for a living, one might have predicted back then that his literary output would be prodigious. Not so. The majority of his short stories, essays, poems, articles, criticism, and other works can fit into a single volume. Poe struggled with writer's block at times, and even when he had to write frequently in his role as an editor of popular magazines, much of what he wrote was tossed-off humour, ephemeral satire and a lot of "marginalia." As a writer, Poe produced some of the most well-remembered, influential and technically innovative work in the history of English literature, some of which even had prophetic and futurist elements (Poe may have been the first to propose a "big bang theory" of the origin of the universe in his book Eureka). However, Poe has also been the favorite target of literary critics and English professors worldwide since the day he died. Every author's body of work includes writing that is beneath their best abilities, but it is unfortunate that much of Poe's oeuvre is throwaway or simply outdated. **Remember:** If Poe can die in abject squalor at 40 and yet be immortalized as an icon of gothic literature, you can also become remembered for your morose personality, your obsession with horror and death, and your passion for impossible romances that are predestined for tragedy, regardless of how little you create. Writing is work: it is therefore to be avoided by every means possible.

Disclaimer: Garth von Buchholz is hoping for some modicum of fame after death. Poe is one of his favorite authors and in 2009 Garth produced the Edgar Allan Poe 200 Project to celebrate Poe's life and work. We are always hardest on the ones we love. ☻

dead pets inspire stories
by H.E. Roulo

"So, tell me what scares you," I memorably said to a room full of innocent people at a dinner party in a suburb of Seattle. It wasn't even my own dinner party. I'm sure they'd remember if I brought it up. Probably. Anyway, it was significant for me, and I remember it vividly because I learned so much.

I'd just completed the podcast of *Fractured Horizon*, my first novel. Confident I finally had time to hone my writing skills, I accepted HorrorAddicts.net's Wicked Women Writers Challenge. My first draft was disappointing, which left me thinking too much and saying too little at the party.

We mingled in groups of two and three, smiled over drinks, and added to murmured conversation. As we cleared the table of empty shrimp tails and broken crackers, I hijacked the conversation.

I caught their attention and asked, "What's your favorite kind of horror?" This topic doesn't fall within Miss Manner's handbook. Did I risk becoming a social reject, uninvited to parties, and an outcast? As dramatic (and sometimes appealing) as that may sound, I remained confident. This topic might even be as good as bringing up dead pets!

In school I'd attended a get-to-know-you mixer, against my will, but was saved from agonizing small talk by a slip of paper with our designated topic of conversation: *Dead Pets!* The conversation that followed was relatable, close to home, and heartfelt. For example, my white teddy-bear hamster, Fluffy, was smarter than any other hamster in the world. He'd escaped his cage and lived off a collection of dry food stolen out of the cats' bowls. We later found his hoard behind the refrigerator. Each night he left his sanctuary to gnaw on my brother's hamster's cage. He almost succeeded in setting her free. Alas, their love was not meant to be.

Anecdotes about our pets and their personalities, capped by their inevitable demise, generated empathy and connection. Sidenote: If you're on a date and lost for topics, dead pets will liven the evening right up.

So, I asked for fears from a room full of innocent dinner guests. My determination to win the first annual Wicked Women Writers Challenge drove me to it. As a long-time science fiction author I needed insight. My first submission attempt, about a character who is beaten and threatened with a gun, wasn't compelling. It certainly wasn't a winner.

At my question, the crowded and well-lit room quieted. Do you know what else comes high on the list of fears? The fear of ridicule. Hesitantly, guests offered common fears: spiders, ghosts, and the return of folk music. The tide turned. Ghoulish dreams and childhood dreads were delightedly confided.

I soon saw that bodily harm alone doesn't make a good story—in any thriller, a body can be sliced by knives and threatened with guns. Horror seeps into dark places of the mind, slides into dreams, and lingers in spidery basements. Horror comes when your *psyche* is in danger.

I compiled my dinner party topic list and narrowed it down to serial killers, live burial, cemeteries, dismemberment, hauntings, and the occult. I added the lingering tension of what is hidden. Horror isn't what you see, it's what you're *about* to see. Tension in the barely-sensed and marginally-understood set the mood for "Graveyard Shift (and Reshift)".

Since then, my palate has become more refined and my horror writing more subtle. Horror is visceral: delightful shivers, skull tightening dread, and the flush of a pounding heartbeat as the moment of discovery draws close. It's anticipation that withholds breath from aching lungs. The horror is coming, but should we uncover our eyes and see what it is? I like my horror full of shadows, so the reader and I peer together into the darkness, not looking too closely.

I no longer use dinner parties to generate story ideas. But I wouldn't be above doing it again, since it worked so well.

I won.

H.E. Roulo is winner of the 2009 Wicked Women Writers Challenge. No pets were harmed in the making of her stories.

hORRoR ReJecTion letters

by StoneslideCorrective

Next time you get a rejection letter, be glad it wasn't one of these.

Dear Writer,

Your manuscript did prove useful in one way. We used it to temporarily sate a very old and always hungry harpy who haunts the moors behind our offices. She feasts on bad writing mixed with the entrails of bats and the bloody paws of bunnies. Please continue to submit, as your work will save us on feed costs.

The Editors

☠☠☠☠☠

Dear Writer,

Greetings from Hell. Your writing doesn't belong here, and we don't want it. Your style is too sweet; your argument is too gentle; and your metaphors are warm-hearted. Plus your logic (innocent), examples (tame). framework, evidence, description, and, basically, everything, are so smarmy and feeble-minded that we doubt even your Earth's *Parade* magazine would accept a mere letter-to-the-editor from you, much less a manuscript.

The Editors

☠☠☠☠☠

Dear Writer,

There are two main problems with your story. First, the human characters all behave like zombies. Second, the zombie characters all behave like kittens.

The Editors

Try the Personalized Rejection Generator at:
stoneslidecorrective.com/rejectionapp

Horror party planning

nightshade on partying

What horror addict doesn't want to plan the perfect party? If you're going to have guests over to your house for a get together, you have a lot to think about. Do you want to decorate with fake blood or real blood? Do you want to use real fingers in your finger sandwiches? How many eyeballs do you want to add to the punch bowl? These are important questions.

Hopefully the articles in this section will help you plan out a great creepy party and your friends will survive to come to another one.

Some tips I've learned are:

☠ Don't serve poisonous punch until the end of the party. Comatose bodies can't play Twister.

☠ Never put out garlic pizza when the vamps are over. You'll never hear the end of it from those drama queens.

☠ Don't invite Frankenstein's monster to a bonfire event. Big mistake! FIRE BAD!

☠ And lastly, if you invite any werewolves, make sure there isn't a full moon out. I made that mistake once and I spent two weeks cleaning up my house. Insurance doesn't cover damage by supernatural creatures. Those jerks! Who doesn't have trouble with werewolves from time to time? Maybe I should start my own insurance company to cover damage from monsters.

pumpkin patch party & Recipes
by Dan Shaurette

Hi, my name is Dan and I am a horror addict. *(Hi Dan!)* I am also a foodie. Just call me the Ghastly Gastronome, or *Ghastronome*. These two passions of mine annually collide headlong around Halloween.

Halloween has been my favorite holiday since childhood. No other holiday combines the celebration of the morbid and macabre with begging for candy! What kid WOULDN'T love that?

When I think of Halloween, I immediately think of Jack-O-Lanterns. Heck, just think of the original posters for the movies *Halloween* and *Halloween II*.

For me, Halloween cooking does mean making fun, creepy goodies, but my real joy is cooking with pumpkin! It seems to me that pumpkin is seriously under-rated. I mean, when Autumn harvests hit, it seems to be all the rage, but in truth, most goodies available are just "pumpkin-spiced". Ask someone to try something other than pumpkin pie, and folks seem to be out of their comfort zone.

Well, I am here to help change all of that, with a plethora of pumpkin recipes straight from the patch.

About Morbid Meals : For the ~~Blood~~ (Food) Is Life

That is the Morbid Meals Manifesto in a nutshell. The better the food, the better the life. I also believe in the converse of this, and that is that the better the life of what you eat, the better the food you eat will be. The fresher the food, the closer you can source it, the better. To put it morbidly, the closer you are to the death of the flora and fauna, the better the food will be.

Baking measurements

Please note that all of the baking recipes here would work best with pastry flour, which has less gluten than All-Purpose flour. Pie crusts, for example, bind up and get tough when there is too much gluten, which is why most crust recipes suggest you work them as little as possible, to avoid binding them up. You can of course make all of these recipes with standard all-purpose flour if you wish.

Whatever flour you choose to use, it is best to *measure by weight*, not by cup volume. Even if you use regular AP flour, measuring by weight gives better turnout because of how you scoop and pack your flour. Volumes can contain different amounts of air, but weight is always the same. So, I highly recommend getting a small, inexpensive digital scale, with measurements in grams and ounces, and a tare button, which allows you to zero out the weight of the bowl you might be using.

Gluten-free Baking

Another reason I give all flour measures by weight and cup is because I personally cook with gluten-free flours. When it comes to GF baking, you do tend to need more flour. Here's a good rule of thumb for making a great, but simple, gluten free flour.

1 cup of AP flour = 140 grams gluten-free flour mix

140 g GF mix = 100 g flour + 40 g starch

For example: 50 g of brown rice flour + 50 g of sweet rice flour + 40 g corn starch

Pumpkin Spice - (from Scratch!)

EXAMINATION

A beginning is a very delicate time. In this time, the most precious substance in the universe is Pumpkin Spice. The Pumpkin Spice extends life and expands consciousness. The Pumpkin Spice is vital to pies, scones, and yes, even lattes. Mmmm… Pumpkin Spice. Definitely my favorite girl power pop singer. She married the footballer, right? Never mind.

ANALYSIS

Ingredients	Apparatus:
2 Tbsp ground cinnamon	Spice grinder (optional, but worth it)
1 Tbsp ground ginger	
2 tsp ground nutmeg	
½ tsp ground allspice	**Yield:**
½ tsp ground cloves	1/4 cup = 4 Tbsp = 12 tsp

PROCEDURE

- If you have a spice grinder, grind your whole dry spices individually. Clean the grinder bowl and cap well with a dry rag between spices.
- Mix together all of the spices and transfer to an airtight container.

DISSECTION

If you don't want to buy a spice grinder, as they can be a bit expensive, a coffee bean grinder works just as well. Electric ones are the best. A spice mill is great for cooking to add spice, but it will not grind fine enough for a mix like this as it is best for cracking.

What about nutmeg? For cooking and wanting to add a light dusting or a pinch of nutmeg to a dish, a nutmeg grater is perfect. But unless you want to grate down a whole nutmeg, you should use a grinder. Just know that you will want to crack the nutmeg (and the cinnamon sticks) first so that they grind easily.

Regarding ginger, if you are grinding that, make sure that you buy dried ginger root, not fresh. Candied ginger is tasty but also not recommended for grinding. Note also that the ginger, believe it or not, was the hardest to grind. Even after breaking it down and grinding longer than the other spices (more than 30 seconds) there were stone-like little balls that refused to grind. Just pick those out and move on.

In my grinding, I found the following measurements to be consistent, but of course, size of any whole spice comes into play:

- One whole nutmeg grinds to about 2 tsp.
- One stick of cinnamon grinds to about 1 Tbsp.
- One piece of dry ginger grinds to about 3 Tbsp.
- The cloves and allspice grounds will compact a bit, so you can grind a little more than what fits in a 1/2 teaspoon.
- If you don't have allspice, you can substitute with 1/2 tsp more of cloves.

Oh, yes. I forgot to tell you... One final word about grinding your own spices. Trust me, do the cloves last. They have the most oil and it stains very well and will flavor the other spices.

POST-MORTEM

He who controls the Pumpkin Spice,
controls the universe. What? Oh, sorry.
Anyway, nothing beats this spice mix when everything is freshly ground. However, if you don't have a grinder or don't want to deal with buying whole spices, then make sure that you buy the best spices you can get.
No matter what, if you make this mix yourself, your dishes will have a consistent, more vibrant flavor than just buying a jar of "pumpkin spice" from the supermarket.
The Pumpkin Spice must flow!

Pumpkin Puree
EXAMINATION

When the craving hits for something made with pumpkin, any old can of pumpkin puree will do the job. However, when the bounty of Autumn's harvest arrives, and there are pumpkins a-plenty, it would be a tragedy of the highest order to not make your own.

ANALYSIS

Ingredients	Apparatus
1 large (about 6 pounds) or 2 small (about 3 pounds) "pie" or "sugar" pumpkins Salt	Baking sheet Food processor, blender, or potato masher
	Yield: 4 cups **Cook Time:** 45 minutes

PROCEDURE

- ☠ Pre-heat your oven to 400°F.

- ☠ Cut off the stem and then split your pumpkin in half from top to bottom.

- ☠ Scoop out all of the fibrous strands, loose pulp, and seeds and set aside for now.

- ☠ Sprinkle the meat with salt and lay the pumpkin halves open-side down on a baking sheet. You can roast them open-face up but I find that dries out the pumpkin too much and doesn't roast as evenly.

- ☠ Roast in your oven for 35 to 45 minutes, until the flesh is fork-tender.

- ☠ While your pumpkin is roasting, clean the pulp and strands off of the seeds by rinsing in some warm water. Save your seeds to roast or bake with later.

- ☠ Remove the pumpkin halves to a cooling rack and allow them to cool down for about an hour.

- ☠ Scoop the roasted meat from the skin into a food processor or blender. Puree until it is completely smooth, about 3 to 4 minutes.

☠ Use immediately in any of the recipes here, or you can keep it refrigerated for up to a week, or freeze it for up to 3 months.

DISSECTION

After Halloween passes is the BEST time to buy pumpkins, in bulk, and then make Pumpkin Puree to store for Thanksgiving and beyond. Pumpkin Puree freezes remarkably well but it isn't recommended that you preserve it. Pumpkin and other squashes are low-acid and even in a pressure canner, it is difficult to get the dense pulp to the proper temperature.

What you can do however is preserve the cubed chunks of pumpkin. One small 3 lb. pumpkin can yield about 2 1/4 lbs. of cubed pumpkin which can be preserved in a quart-sized jar. Follow your pressure canner's instructions. Then when ready to make into puree, be sure to drain all of the water and roast as directed above.

POST-MORTEM

Pumpkin Puree is used in the bulk of the following recipes. As such, the fresher your puree, the fresher your treats will taste. I won't judge you if you opt for buying the cans, but at least once, you should try making your own. I think you'll agree, when pumpkins are in season, there's nothing better.

Perfect Pie Crust

EXAMINATION

Making your own crust from scratch may seem intimidating, but with just a little patience, it is very rewarding. "Blind baking" your crust makes all the difference in having a perfectly flaky and still tender crust that holds up to the filling.

ANALYSIS

Ingredients	Apparatus
6 Tbsp unsalted butter, chilled	Food processor or pastry cutter
2 Tbsp lard or shortening, chilled	1 pound of pie weights or dried beans
1 1/2 cup pastry flour (170g/6oz)	Aluminum foil or parchment paper
1/2 tsp salt	Plastic cling wrap
1/2 tsp sugar	9-inch pie pan
1 tsp Pumpkin Spice (optional)	Rolling pin
	Yield: 1 9-inch pie crust
3 Tbsp ice water	**Cook Time:** 25 minutes

PROCEDURE

☠ Freeze the butter and lard/shortening for 15 minutes.

☠ Into your food processor, add all of your dry ingredients, and pulse a few times until well combines.

☠ Take your butter and fat from your freezer and cut it all up into small pieces. Add the butter and fat together to the food processor and pulse to combine. The dough should start to form small pea-sized clumps.

☠ Add the water a tablespoon at a time to the food processor and pulse a few times. Repeat as needed until the dough comes together when squeezed between your fingers.

☠ Take the dough from the food processor and form it gently into a ball. Wrap the dough ball in plastic wrap and gently flatten into a round disk. Place the wrapped disk of dough in your pie pan into your refrigerator for at least 30 minutes. (At this point you could also just freeze the disk of dough for up to 3 months!)

☠ Sprinkle your work surface and rolling pin with flour. Remove your dough from the fridge and unwrap.

☠ Roll out your dough, working from the center out to the edge, until you have a circle about 11 to 12 inches wide.

☠ Remove your pie pan from the fridge and carefully transfer your rolled dough to the inside of the pie pan. Trim and crimp the edges as needed. Place the dough back into the refrigerator for 15 more minutes.

☠ In your oven, set a rack in the middle position and preheat to 425°F.

☠ Remove the pie pan with the dough from the refrigerator. Line the inside of the dough with a sheet of parchment paper or aluminum foil. Pour the pie weights (or dry beans) on top and make sure to press into the edges and sides of the lining. Bake in the oven for 10 to 12 minutes, until the edges just start to turn golden brown.

☠ Remove the lining and weights and then continue to bake the crust until it is dry and just becoming golden brown, about 5 to 10 more minutes.

☠ Remove the blind-baked crust from the oven and allow it to cool completely.

DISSECTION

If you can't find pastry flour, a 50/50 mix of cake flour and all-purpose flour works well. Of course, if all that you have on hand is all-purpose, then you can use that, just remember not to over work the dough.

☠☠☠☠☠☠☠

POST-MORTEM

Okay, I'll admit it. The most important trick to making the "perfect" pie crust is practice. With everything, practice makes, well... perfect. *Eventually*. Don't beat yourself up too much if the dough cracks, is too thin, too thick, too dry, crumbles, etc. This is especially true of gluten-free pie crusts. Feel free to experiment with getting the ratios right.

Pumpkin Pie
EXAMINATION

Once upon a time, I did not like Pumpkin Pie. After I discovered the best way to make the Perfect Pie Crust, the battle was won but the war still raged on. Besides a soggy crust, the other tragedy of most pumpkin pie is the canned pie filling. By this I specifically mean the pumpkin pie filling that is already spiced, has added sugar, and other frankly unnecessary ingredients. Oh, and don't even get me started on the condensed milk.

Canned 100% pumpkin puree however is better for making a pie with because you have full control over the ingredients and flavors. If you want the freshest pie you've ever had, then consider making your own Pumpkin Puree. Not all pumpkins are the same, nor are they always in season. Canned pumpkin puree always seems to be available and ready to use.

Finally, there's the Pumpkin Spice. Always use the best spices for the pie. I recommend combining your own mix instead of buying some mega-mart jar. Even better is grinding it yourself, if you have the equipment and inclination. The difference in flavor with fresh ground spices is dramatically better.

ANALYSIS

Ingredients	Apparatus
2 cups Pumpkin Puree	Large saucepan
1 cup half-and-half	Large mixing bowl
2 Tbsp Pumpkin Spice	A 9-inch pie pan
1/2 tsp salt	
2 large eggs	**Servings:** 8
1 cup dark brown sugar	**Yield:** 1 9-inch pie
	Cook Time: 50 minutes

PROCEDURE

☠ In a large saucepan, simmer the Pumpkin Puree over medium heat for about 2 to 3 minutes.

- ☠ Add the half-and-half, Pumpkin Spice, and salt to the pumpkin, then return to a simmer for another 2 to 3 minutes. When the pumpkin mixture is thick and not runny, remove from heat and allow to cool.
- ☠ Pre-heat your oven at 350°F.
- ☠ In a large bowl, whisk the eggs and then whisk in the brown sugar.
- ☠ Combine the pumpkin mixture and egg mixture together.
- ☠ Pour the filling into a blind-baked Pie Crust.
- ☠ Bake the pie until the filling is set, about 45 to 50 minutes.
- ☠ Remove the pie to a cooling rack and allow to cool for at least two hours before serving.

DISSECTION

As a wonderful variation, I sometimes substitute the cup of brown sugar with 1/2 cup of pure maple syrup. The real deal; not that flavored corn syrup on the breakfast aisle.

POST-MORTEM

Those are the big secrets to Pumpkin Pie. It's really all about a pre-baked, or "blind baked" crust, fresh pumpkin and the best spices you can get. No longer will you be covering your pie in shame with mounds of whipped cream.

how to hull pumpkin seeds

EXAMINATION

Like other edible seeds, you can eat pumpkin seeds with the white hull still on them, or you can crack them open to enjoy the green seeds inside. When these green seeds are prepared to be eaten, they are called *pepitas*. They can be found in most markets about as often as the whole ones can be.

ANALYSIS

Ingredients	Apparatus
Fresh pumpkins	Large knife
Water	Large spoon
Salt	Strainer
	Waxed or parchment paper
Yield: 1 cup	Rolling pin
	Large pot

PROCEDURE

☠ Cut your pumpkin in half, or carve up like a jack-o-lantern.

☠ Scoop out the seeds and sticky fibrous pulp into a strainer.

☠ Clean the seeds by running warm water over them. Gently pick out or push through the unwanted pulp.

☠ Lay the seeds out flat on a sheet of waxed or parchment paper. Let the seeds dry completely.

☠ Use a rolling pin to flatten the seeds just enough to crack the shells. Depending on how many you have, you could just pick the pepitas out.

☠ If you have a lot of seeds, then fill a large pot with water, about two cups of water for every cup of seeds. Bring the water to a boil.

☠ Pour the pumpkin seeds into the boiling water and cover the pot with a lid. Boil the seeds for up to 30 minutes. The cracked hulls will float to the top while the pepitas sink to the bottom.

- ☠ Remove the pot from the heat and uncover it. Using your strainer, or a slotted spoon, scoop out all of the floating hulls.
- ☠ After all of the hulls are removed, pour the water and seeds into your strainer. Rinse in cold water to stop them from continuing to cook.
- ☠ Lay the seeds out flat again onto some waxed or parchment paper and let them dry out.

DISSECTION

This really is a very quick process. Don't let all of the steps overwhelm you. It is also totally worthwhile. Sure, you could eat the white hull, but these are so much better with that removed.

POST-MORTEM

Pepitas make excellent brittle candy, and candied pepitas are a great alternative to roasted pumpkin seeds. I like to have pepitas candied or just roasted.

pepita brittle

Nut brittles are a Halloween classic, but they are great all year round. I typically only find peanut brittle, or an occasional cashew brittle perchance. With the availability of pepitas (pumpkin seeds with the white hulls removed) there's no reason not to try a little variety.

ANALYSIS

Ingredients	Apparatus
1 1/2 cups lightly salted, roasted pepitas	Medium-sized saucepan with a llid
1 tsp Pumpkin Spice	Wooden spoon
1/4 tsp cayenne pepper (optional)	Spatula
3 cups sugar	Baking sheet pan lined with parchment paper
1 1/2 cups water	
Vegetable oil or non-stick spray	**Servings:** 16
	Yield: 4 cups

PROCEDURE

☠ Grease the inside of the saucepan with oil or non-stick spray. Do the same to your spatula and set aside.

☠ Add the sugar and water, and bring to a boil over high heat. Stir occasionally with the wooden spoon.

☠ Once it starts to boil, cover with the lid and cook for 3 minutes.

☠ Remove the lid and bring the heat down to medium. Cook until the sugar is light amber in color.

☠ Stir in the pepitas and spices, and incorporate quickly and completely.

☠ Pour the mixture onto a parchment paper-lined baking sheet. Spread thin with the greased spatula. Allow the brittle to cool completely.

☠ Once cooled and hard, break into pieces.

DISSECTION

While you can absolutely make this recipe with fresh pepitas, and I hope you will, you can absolutely use pepitas from your local bulk whole foods store. If your local grocery store has a well-stocked Mexican food section, they may also sell pepitas there.

Note, there is NO corn syrup used at all in this recipe. Corn syrup is EVIL, and quite frankly unnecessary.

Note also that you do not need a candy thermometer. They are useful, of course, but the telltale sign of the syrup turning amber is all the indication you need.

POST-MORTEM

I think I love breaking the brittle apart just a little more than eating it. How about you? Do be careful though, some pieces can be sharp.

It keeps pretty well, too. Stored in an airtight container, pepita brittle can last up to two weeks. Assuming you don't eat it all day one.

Candied Pepitas

EXAMINATION

Looking for an alternative to roasted pumpkin seeds? Look no further than this sweet and spicy treat.

ANALYSIS

Ingredients	Apparatus
2 tsp butter	Large frying pan
1/2 cup hulled raw	Serving plate or waxed
pumpkin seeds	paper covered baking sheet
1/2 tsp Pumpkin Spice	
1/8 tsp cayenne (optional)	**Yield:** 1/2 cup
1/8 tsp salt	
1 Tbsp honey	

PROCEDURE

☠ In a large frying pan, melt the butter over medium heat.

☠ Add the pumpkin seeds, pumpkin spice, cayenne, and salt, then stir until seeds begin to brown, about 2 minutes.

☠ Add the honey and stir for another minute.

☠ Remove from heat and spread the seeds out onto a plate or waxed paper covered baking sheet.

☠ Allow the seeds to cool for at least 15 minutes, making sure they are not sticky.

DISSECTION

These can keep in an airtight container for up to 3 days, but be sure to use them as soon as possible. Do not refrigerate or freeze as they will gum up from condensation.

POST-MORTEM

As healthy snacks go, you can't get much better than candied pepitas. They are also great on salads, in cookies and other baked goods, and more! Like Pepita Brittle...

Maple Pumpkin Ice Cream

EXAMINATION

So what do you do when it is Autumn but it is still warm out and you want a cool treat? You make pumpkin ice cream of course!

ANALYSIS

Ingredients	Apparatus
4 large eggs	Ice Cream maker
1 cup brown sugar	Large bowl
1 quart heavy or whipping cream	Whisk or egg
2 cup milk	beater
1/2 cup maple syrup	
2 cup Pumpkin Puree	Yield: 2 quarts
1 Tbsp Pumpkin Spice	
1/2 cup Candied Pepitas or Pecan	
Pralines (optional)	

PROCEDURE

1. Beat the eggs in a large bowl until light and fluffy.
2. Add the brown sugar in small amounts and whisk together until completely combined.
3. Add in the remaining ingredients, except the nuts, and whisk together until completely combined.
4. Pour mixture into ice cream maker's canister. Chill the canister in the refrigerator for 30 minutes.
5. Setup your ice cream maker per instructions and start churning.
6. If adding in nuts, fold them into the ice cream when the ice cream machine starts to slow down.

DISSECTION

It is possible to make this without a machine. Instead, you will need a 2 quart freezer-safe container with a lid. Just pour your mixture into that and cover tightly with the lid. Place the container into your freezer and let it freeze until firm, at least 4 hours. You might want to stir it every hour. Not aggressively but enough to make sure it freezes evenly.

☠☠☠☠☠☠

POST-MORTEM

I love this stuff. It is like frozen Autumn.

Pumpkin Butter

EXAMINATION

Pumpkin "butter" is kind of a deceiving name for this aromatic ambrosia. Rather, this is more of a sweet sauce made of pumpkin, spices, all-natural juices, and syrups.

ANALYSIS

Ingredients	Apparatus
2 cups Pumpkin Puree	Large saucepan
1/2 cup apple juice, no sugar added	
1/2 cup honey	**Yield:** 2 cups
2 Tbsp pure maple syrup	
1 Tbsp Pumpkin Spice	
1 tsp molasses	
1 tsp lemon juice	
pinch salt	

PROCEDURE

☠ Place all of the ingredients in a large saucepan over high heat and stir well to combine.

☠ Bring the mixture to a boil. Reduce heat to low and simmer for 30 minutes or until thickened to your taste. Stir occasionally to prevent burning around the edges.

☠ Allow the mixture to cool before pouring into a jar or container.

☠ Let it set in the refrigerator overnight so that all of the flavors to really meld together and thicken up.

DISSECTION

If you have a crock pot then you can get your slow cooking on. Just set to Low and cook for 2 to 3 hours. If you want to double the recipe to make more (because this stuff is incredible!) make sure that you double the time to slow cook to about 4 to 5 hours.

If you do not have a crock pot, you can still slow cook this if you have a casserole dish with an oven safe lid, or a dutch oven. Just bake in an oven set to 200 F degrees for the same amount of time.

This stuff smells and tastes great, so I go the stovetop route personally.

As with Pumpkin Puree, Pumpkin Butter freezes very well but it isn't recommended that you preserve Pumpkin Butter. Pumpkin and other squashes are low-acid and even though this is cooked thoroughly with apple and lemon juice, it may not approach the proper pH level for pressure canning. Botulism is a nasty thing, my friends.

POST-MORTEM
This is delicious on everything, but it goes especially well with pumpkin scones and pound cake.

Pumpkin Scones

EXAMINATION

Pumpkin scones and clotted cream. What better breakfast or tea snack could there possibly be? None, I dare say.

ANALYSIS

Ingredients	For The Spiced Glaze
2 cups flour (227g/8oz)	1 cup powdered sugar
1/2 cup brown sugar, packed	1 tsp Pumpkin Spice
1 Tbsp Pumpkin Spice	2 Tbsp milk
1 tsp baking powder	1/4 tsp vanilla extract
1/2 tsp baking soda	
1/4 tsp salt	**For The Icing**
1/2 cup (1 stick) unsalted butter, cubed	1 cup powdered sugar
1/2 cup Pumpkin Puree	2 Tbsp milk
3 Tbsp half & half or whole milk	
1 large egg	**Optional**
2 tsp vanilla extract	1/2 cup Candied Pepitas

Apparatus

Baking sheet
2 Large bowls
Whisk
Rubber spatula
Pizza cutter or large knife
Rolling pin
Parchment paper (optional)

Yield: 8 scones
Cook Time: 15 minutes

PROCEDURE

☠ Preheat your oven to 400°F, and place one rack in the middle of your oven.

☠ If you have parchment paper, line a baking sheet and set aside.

☠ In a large mixing bowl, mix your flour, sugar, spices, baking powder, baking soda, and salt.

- ☠ Add small pieces of the chilled butter to the dry ingredients and combine with a pastry cutter, or use a food processor with quick pulses. The dough should start to form small clumps of crumbs.
- ☠ In another large mixing bowl, mix the Pumpkin Puree, milk, eggs, and vanilla extract. Add this wet mixture to the dry ingredients and combine until a dough forms.
- ☠ Lightly dust flour on a working surface, then dump out the dough on that floured surface and knead the dough, only until it comes together well. Place the dough onto the baking sheet and roll it out to about an inch thick.
- ☠ For a gluten-free version, chill the dough for 30 minutes as you won't be able to knead it. Don't roll it out either, just press it down to about an inch thick.
- ☠ Cut into eight slices like a pie.
- ☠ Place the baking sheet into the oven and bake at 400°F for about 10 to 12 minutes.
- ☠ Remove from oven and place scones on a cooling rack.
- ☠ To make the icing, whisk together the powdered sugar and milk until smooth.
- ☠ To make the spiced glaze, whisk together the powdered sugar, pumpkin spice, vanilla, and milk.
- ☠ Let the scones cool for at least 10 minutes. Drizzle on the spiced glaze, sprinkle with candied pepitas, then drizzle on icing.

DISSECTION

Serve these scones warm with clotted or whipped cream and Pumpkin Butter.

POST-MORTEM

Die happy knowing such joy. In your mouth.

Pumpkin Raisin Cookies

EXAMINATION

P is for Pumpkin. That's good enough for me. I suppose if you were going to feed a monster around Halloween, one that eats Pumpkin Raisin Cookies would be a delightful change of pace.

ANALYSIS

Ingredients	Apparatus
1 cup flour (120g/4.25oz)	Cookie sheet
2/3 cup old-fashioned oats	Parchment paper (optional)
2 tsp Pumpkin Spice	Two mixing bowls
1/2 tsp baking soda	
1/2 tsp salt	**Servings:** 24
3/4 cup sugar, plus	**Cook Time:** 20 minutes
additional for sprinkling	
1/2 cup Pumpkin Puree	
1/3 cup vegetable oil	
1 Tbsp pure maple syrup	
1 tsp vanilla extract	
1/2 cup raisins	

PROCEDURE

- Preheat your oven to 350°F, and place one rack in the middle of the oven.
- If you have parchment paper, line a cookie sheet and set aside.
- In a mixing bowl, mix the flour, oats, spices, baking soda, and salt.
- In another bowl, mix the sugar, Pumpkin Puree, oil, maple syrup, and vanilla extract.
- Combine the dry ingredients with the wet mixture, then add the raisins.
- Scoop the cookie dough into balls roughly an inch around and place on the cookie sheet about an inch apart. Sprinkle with sugar.
- Bake the cookies at 350°F for 18 to 20 minutes.
- Move the cookies to a cooling rack.

DISSECTION
These cookies are fantastic with a gluten-free flour. Even if you don't have a gluten or wheat sensitivity, I find that gluten-free flours make crispier, crunchier cookies. With the pumpkin in this mix, they will come out chewy, too, which is quite nice.

POST-MORTEM
Omigosh, like forget that crazy sock puppet! I'm keeping these all to myself. *Nom-nom-nom!*

Pumpkin Pound Cake

EXAMINATION

I almost didn't include this recipe. I mean we've got pie, scones, and cookies. Do you really need pound cake, too? Yes. Yes, you do. Especially Pumpkin Pound Cake. Worth the price of this book alone!

ANALYSIS

Ingredients	For The Spiced Glaze
1 1/2 cup sugar	1 cup powdered sugar
1/2 cup vanilla yogurt	1 tsp Pumpkin Spice
3 large eggs	2 Tbsp milk
1 cup Pumpkin Puree	1/4 tsp vanilla extract
1 1/2 cup cake flour	**Apparatus**
(170g/6oz)	Loaf pan (at least 8 1/2"x4
1 tsp Pumpkin Spice	1/2")
1/2 tsp salt	Large mixing bowl
1/2 tsp baking soda	
1/2 tsp baking powder	Servings: 8

PROCEDURE

- Grease up the sides of your loaf pan and set it aside.
- Preheat your oven to 350°F.
- In a large mixing bowl, whisk together the sugar, yogurt, and eggs.
- Add the pumpkin puree and stir together.
- Add the remaining dry ingredients and mix well.
- Pour the batter into the loaf pan and bake at 350°F for 60 minutes.
- When the cake is done, remove to a cooling rack.
- While the cake cools, make the spiced glaze by whisking together the powdered sugar, pumpkin spice, vanilla, and milk.
- Let the cake cool for at least 10 minutes, then drizzle on the spiced glaze.

DISSECTION

If you prefer the southern-style of a pound cake in a Bundt cake pan, a small 7 1/2-inch pan will work. For a large 10-

inch Bundt pan, you can double the recipe to accommodate.

You can use low-fat or fat-free vanilla yogurt, if you want to reduce the fat in the cake. You could also use just egg whites instead of whole eggs.

POST-MORTEM

You will be the Belle of the Ball if you take this glazed cake to your next Halloween potluck. You might even want to make two. Because cake.

Pumpkin-Spiced Latte

EXAMINATION

We all know Spring has arrived when the Groundhog can't
see his shadow. How do we know Autumn has arrived?
Why the brewing of the Pumpkin-Spiced Latte, of course.

ANALYSIS

Ingredients	Apparatus
3 Tbsp strong ground coffee	"Tall" coffee cup (12 oz)
3/4 cup water	Coffee maker
1/2 tsp Pumpkin Spice	Microwave safe cup or measuring cup
2 tsp honey	Immersion blender or whisk
3/4 cup milk (any kind)	
	Servings: 1
	Yield: 1 tall cup (12 oz)

PROCEDURE

1. Brew your coffee based on your maker's instructions, using the coffee and water.
2. In your tall coffee cup, pour in your honey and spices, and stir to combine.
3. While the coffee brews, steam your milk in a microwave oven for 10-15 seconds, or simmer in a saucepan over medium heat just until it starts to boil. Remove from heat.
4. Carefully whisk or blend the hot milk until it has a frothy head, about 2 or 3 minutes.
5. When the coffee is done, pour the coffee into your tall coffee cup, then stir to combine with spiced honey. Pour in the milk, then spoon the foam on top. Sprinkle with a dash of Pumpkin Spice.

DISSECTION

The drink as prepared is an even ratio between milk and
coffee. Many have debated whether it should be 2:1 in
favor of coffee to milk, or a shot of espresso with cup then
filled with steamed milk. The foam of course is also
optional. I'll leave such battles as an exercise for the reader.

POST-MORTEM

I personally don't drink much coffee, and I no longer buy it from chain coffeehouses because it is frankly just too expensive. With this recipe, I can enjoy it anytime the craving hits.

Pumpkin-Spiced Mulled Cider

EXAMINATION

There may be no drink that evokes a season quite so much as mulled cider. If you think it is only a Yuletide drink, though, try this Pumpkin-spiced version and you'll find that Autumn has met its match.

ANALYSIS

Ingredients	Apparatus
2 quarts apple cider	Large saucepan or slow cooker
1 apple, quartered	
1/4 cup brown sugar, packed	
	Servings: 8
1/2 tsp Pumpkin Spice	Yield: 8 cups
2 whole cinnamon sticks	
6 whole cloves	

PROCEDURE

1. In a large saucepan, combine all of the ingredients.
2. Cover and heat on low for 15 to 20 minutes.
3. Remove cinnamon sticks, cloves, and apple pieces before serving.

DISSECTION

If you have a 3-quart slow cooker/crock pot you can use that and cook it covered on a low setting for 2 hours. This is great for making your whole house smell like fall, but I personally find it makes me too impatient, so I prefer the stovetop method.

💀💀💀💀💀💀💀

POST-MORTEM

Mulled cider is something I typically drink in the winter, but when it tastes like pumpkin spice, it helps me pretend it is only Autumn, and then I'm not freezing so much. This makes a great alternative to the Pumpkin-Spiced Latte for those that don't like coffee.

hoSTinG a CReepy CRawly paRTy

by Chantal Boudreau

DISCLAIMER: While the things described in this article are real, they are to be used at your own risk—especially the exploding insects. And I don't really endorse scaring the bejeezers out of grandma with rubber critters. That's pretty risky too.

Plenty of people have heard of creepy crawly theme parties for Halloween. You know the ones—snacks include gummy worms and brains, chocolate pretzel spiders, peeled grape eyeballs, lady finger cookies, and ants on a log celery sticks? These are the same parties offering up games like "What's in the bag?" where you shove your hands into gross-feeling bag contents that are usually things like soggy spaghetti or some other sticky or gloopy thing. And party favours might involve rubber bugs or splat hands with a booger-like texture that adhere to the wall when you fling them. These parties are cute and silly, but not exactly scary. They aren't the type of party that would appeal to a *true* horror addict.

So how then can you frighten up a creepy crawly party to give it authentic and dramatic horror appeal? I'm talking ways to add a real bite to your fright. Be aware, my suggestions aren't intended for the faint of heart. If creepy crawlies make your stomach turn and your skin crawl, this kind of party certainly isn't for you.

Let's start with party snacks. If you want to offer some edible scare with flair, why stop at fake insects for the eating. Think I'm joking? No more so than my local Natural History Museum's "cooking with bugs" programming, or the recipes I dug up while researching my arachnophobic short story "Octavia" which appears in Crooked Cat's charity anthology, *Fear: Volume I*. I discovered that in Cambodia, spiders are sometimes consumed—even baked into cookies. Apparently, they taste like peanut butter (not that I've tried them myself, although I've had a taste of pan-fried mealworm. Mmmm, crunchy goodness.)

Not willing to scour the world wide web in search of spidery dishes? You're in luck. You can get yourself a copy of *The Eat-a-Bug Cookbook* by David George Gordon or *Top 50 Most Delicious Insect Recipes* by Julie Hatfield instead, so that you have a selection of those recipes readily available in one handy book.

Not much of a cook? Have no fear, or rather, have extra fear. That's the point of all this, after all. You can buy pre-assembled buggy snacks care of Hotlix. They offer a variety of insect centres to their confectionaries. You'll find cricket lick-its, ant candy with real farm ants, scorpion suckers, and a variety of chocolate-flavoured insects. They also have crick-ette and larvet worm snax for the diabetics in your crowd. These are all snacks that will put the gummy worms and peeled grapes to shame.

How about party favours? Rubber bugs and snakes are fun for a cheap scare at grandma's expense, but their value and entertainment life is short-lived. If you want a party favour with a longer-lasting gross factor, consider buying your party favours from the Real Insect Company. They carry pens, bottle openers, paperweights, bracelets, key chains, and necklaces containing a selection of real creepy crawlies from yellow jackets to scorpions. They even have real vampire bats in their more extravagant desk decorations.

Want entertainment to match your theme? Aside from letting loose your sister's pet snake, rats or tarantula and watching how fast your guests scatter, here are a few other suggestions how you can keep your creepy-crawly party rolling.

Show your guests some creepy crawly-movies. An oldie favourite like *The Fly*, *Ben* or *Them* offers some shivery thrills, or something with B-movie homage like *Slither* might be more to your taste. Horror-movies.ca has a top ten list of creepy crawly movies you can choose from if you don't have any ideas of your own.

Next, you could read them a scary story or two, a la camp-out fireside chiller. You'll find plenty of possibilities in May December Publications' *Spiders* anthology or choice morsels in their *Midnight Movie Creature Feature* anthologies (Wrigglers can make your guests squirm if told with the proper panache.) Turn the lights down low and get your spook on.

Party music? Check out <u>virtualdreamer.com</u>'s *Blue Bayou Relaxation Sounds*. You can serenade your guests with real sounds of crickets, frogs, and bugs. Not so scary, but it does match the theme.

And when the day is done and it's time to go, send your guests off with a blast. Never mind backyard friendly fireworks. To inspire them to run, how about a sampling of exploding bugs—Camponotus saundersi (exploding ants), Globitermes sulphureus (exploding termite), and Acyrthosiphon pisum (the exploding pea aphid)—ewwww.

They may not all make it home alive, but for the ones who do, your authentic creepy-crawly themed party will be one your guests will never forget.

October Dreaming

by David Watson

When you think of favorite months for horror addicts, you have to think of October. There is so much to love about the month. Leaves are changing, lots of good horror movies are on TV, and of course the month ends in a holiday that celebrates our passion, Halloween. Some people don't wait until October 31st to celebrate Halloween, they start their celebration in the summer.

The summer is when home haunters are planning and building their haunts that will be open for the whole month of October. Also, the people who run haunted attractions are hiring people to build their sets and finding haunt actors to scare the thousands of people who will be going through their haunted location.

Haunt actors are a special breed of actors. All year long they think of ways to scare customers and when the weather starts to get cold, their only wish is to make you scream in terror. Haunt actors look normal when they're not working, but when they go to work, they have makeup artists and costume people who get them ready to scare the pants off of anyone who is foolish enough to enter their domain. It's hard work being a haunt actor. At the end of the night, your throat hurts from yelling, you're exhausted from chasing victims in your area, and occasionally you have to put the extra effort in to scare the people who think they can't be scared. I've worked in haunts for a couple of years and the last two years my son has worked at a haunted house and has some good insight into haunt acting as well. Below are seven tips for being a good haunt actor.

☠ **Know your area:** Most haunts are divided into separate rooms. It's a good idea to know where your victims will be entering and exiting. Know where the dark corners are so you can hide yourself and keep the element of surprise. Remember to work with the actors in your area. With a little teamwork anyone who goes through your area will want to run home to their mommy.

☠ **Create a story:** Does your area have a theme? If not, you and the other actors in your area should come up with one. Of course, you can just jump out and scare people, but if you want them to remember who you are, you need to be creative. For instance, having two actors playing zombies and eating a third actor while he screams out in pain is a good, simple idea. You can then have another actor come in for the scare as the customers watch the feeding frenzy.

☠ **Know your character:** If you're a zombie, take some time and think. How does a zombie walk? What noises do they make? How do they move their arms? What do they sound like? Practice what you think they would be like and when you're acting in the haunt, don't let your customers see you out of character.

☠ **Think of a few scary songs and phrases:** Catch phrases are a good thing to make people remember you. "Your head would look great mounted on my wall", or "If you want to keep breathing you better stop screaming" are great haunt phrases. You can take a popular song and turning it into something spooky is something that works. Lyrics from "Frosty the Snowman" can become "Andrew the salesman, I ate him from a bowl, I shredded his stomach and ate his toes, and then wiped my nose."

- **Stare at people:** Something as simple as staring at people really gets a reaction. No one wants to be stared at, but when you're going through a haunted house you're basically asking for it. Looking right at a person and showing no emotion is enough to set someone on edge and they will keep thinking of you in their nightmares.
- **If you hear a victim's name in a haunted house make sure you use it:** People scare easy when the monster is saying their name, the customer will be scared and embarrassed because it's like they're being singled out. If you can get all the monsters in the haunt to use their name, it makes it that much better.
- **Let your inner psycho out:** This is your chance to be as crazy as you want to be. You're supposed to be scary, so act that way. Move your arms, scream a lot, overact, and be psychotic. People who come up to you in a haunt want to be scared, so you have to deliver and since you're probably under a lot of makeup or a costume you can be as wild as you want to be.

Keep in mind, being a haunt actor is an art form. People don't do this for the money, they do it because they love it. If you like to scare people, wear fake blood, and dress up in a creepy costume. Then you will enjoy being a haunt actor.

A haunt isn't the only place where you can dress up and let your inner ghoul out. You can find several horror conventions throughout the year where you can dress up and find people who share your passion. Halloween costumes aren't just for kids. For haunt actors and convention goers, they're more like a way of life.

bloody Good Party Games

by Emerian Rich

☠ BLOODY MURDER WORD GAME

When I was a little girl at the store with my mom and I wanted to look at the toys while my mom was on another aisle, her instructions were. "Be careful and if a stranger comes near you, scream bloody murder." Boy was the unsuspecting adult who innocently wandered into my aisle surprised when I took one look at her and screamed, "BLOODY MURDER!" Yeah, I was a literal kinda kid. Now, you can use my childish faux pas at your next party. This game requires pen and paper. Give your guests the phrase "Bloody Murder" and see how many words they can think of that contain those letters. Give them 1-2 minutes to think and when time is up, scream, "BLOODY MURDER!" The guest with the most words, wins.

HARDCORE ADDICT STYLE - Don't tell them you are going to scream and when time is up, scare the hell out of all of them by screaming, "BLOODY MURDER!"*

☠ PIN THE ARM ON THE...Zombie? Frankie? Skeleton? Vampire?

No doubt you've picked up a Halloween ornament through the years that just won't stay dead. The adjustable "body" (the zombie, skeleton, etc that has limbs attached by brads so that they are adjustable) is one of those that even though their leg or arm or head comes off, you doctor it up with tape year after year until the once adjustable limbs are frozen up like rigamortis has set in. Why not take one of your older pieces and offer it up as a sacrifice to the party gods this year? Detach a leg, arm, or head from your weathered friend and put the rest of his body up on a

225

bill board or on a wall if you are using tape. Then, blindfold your friends one by one and let them "pin" the body part to the body. The person with the best blindfolded aim, wins.

HARDCORE ADDICT STYLE - Blindfold all your friends at once and let them use stickpins... first person to bleed goes for a beer run.*

☠ DARLING IF YOU LOVE...

This is a spin on a classic game played in my family for generations. The object? To make your friends and family laugh. The one who doesn't laugh or smile is the winner, but that rarely happens. People sit around the room where they can all see each other. One to go first must approach someone in the room and say, "Darling if you love <u>vampires</u>, please don't smile." The word <u>vampires</u> can be swapped out for any other horror icon. Werewolves, Frankenstein's monster, squidmen, ghosts, black cats, etc... The catch is, while saying the phrase, you must act like the creature you are stating. For instance, if you say werewolves, you could add a howl to the end of the phrase. If you say ghosts, you can "oooohhhhhh" out your words. There is no touching and everyone else in the room may laugh at will, so your acting skills are what will make the person laugh, or not. There is really no winner in this game, it goes on until everyone's had a chance to make a fool of themselves.

HARDCORE ADDICT STYLE - Using props is always a nice choice, but remember - no touching!*

☠ PASS THE BODY PART

Every self-respecting horror addict I know has a spare body part laying around the house. Whether it be a plastic skull, a rubber leg stump, or a sticky ear toy, you can find something in your home to play this game with. If you've used all those for decor, grab a pile of grapes and peel... they make for a great eyeball feel. Set up chairs in a circle and click on your favorite spooky tunes. For me, I like Midnight Syndicate's *Monsters of Legend* CD or the 1931 *Dracula* music by Philip Glass. Start the music and pass the body part. When you stop the music, the person holding the body part wins, or loses depending on your view point.

HARDCORE ADDICT STYLE - Blindfold all your friends and have them pass the "eyeball" around. Don't tell them it's really a grape.*

*HorrorAddicts.net is not responsible for any heart attacks, bleeding wounds, friend freak-outs, or unstoppable laugher needing medical assistance that may occur while playing. Discretion is advised.

horror fashion

nightshade on fashion

Listen up addicts because this is a very important section. I may not seem like a gal who takes my appearance seriously, but it takes a lot of work to make it look this effortless. Despite my style, we all need help with our make-up and outfits sometimes and this section should give you some real good ideas. The most important thing, though, is to always be yourself when you dress up. The first person you need to impress is you.

As addicts, we hang out with a myriad of people who dress in different styles. In our world, it's not that odd to see a punk, goth, and pin-up together. We also embrace those who dress like norms, but have a bloody horror center. The horror flick T-shirt crew is welcome too.

The point is, you should never dress to make other people happy. I also think it's a good idea to carry accessories. For instance, people may not like what you're wearing (which is okay) but you should carry something special for the rude ones. You know, the ones that stare, laugh, or say something mean. I keep a little utility belt on and carry things like mace, poison, and a little knife. I figure, if they want to take the time to complain, I can take the time to give them something to complain about.

fashion top 10
by Mimielle

1. A GOOD Black Eyeliner for everyone! Yes Guyliner is bigger than ever! (Gel crayons double as lip liner, I'm a fan...)

2. SUNSCREEN. Even if you don't maintain a gothic pallor, protecting your skin keeps it more beautiful.

3. A pair of staples are A) A good hair product to tame or fluff your hair and define your style and B) A BB or CC cream, with skin benefits and good coverage. For guys who don't use makeup, a colorless but mattifying foundation primer is undetectable on the skin but has skin benefits and works some pore-vanishing magic!

4. A staple black bottom piece. Black skirt, jeans, leggings, bondage pants, cargo pants/shorts. It's the most versatile thing in your wardrobe and the easiest to change as a seasonal trend piece!

5. Favorite fandom T-shirt(s). Whether it's a band shirt, vintage horror movie tie-in or blackletter gym, club or coffee shop shirt, REPRESENT your alternative interests by displaying them once in a while. Extra points if it's somehow distressed, laced or bleach-'dyed'. Get creative!

6. A black or white button-down shirt. You can wear it so many ways! Over T's and tanks, under vests and sweaters, tucked or untucked. I use a men's pleated tuxedo shirt that I stole from my swain.

7. One or two unusual pieces or trademark 'you' looks. For example a couple of mine are 'all white and pale with intense lips and eyes' and 'all black but frilly and with heavy makeup' and I build most of my wardrobe around these kinds of looks.

8. A go-to 'uniform'. A set of clothes and a practiced makeup look that you can throw together in very minimal time and always look fab. Mine is a black TrippNYC dress, blow drying my hair straight and a winged black liner/red lip look. Out the door in 20 (shh, don't tell!)

9. A great pair of boots or shoes. Docs, Demonia Buckle Boots, your trusty Converse Chucks. Keep them polished/neat even if your look is more deconstructed/grunge.

10. A fierce attitude! Confidence is ultimately the key to pulling off any look!

Goth Fashion Favorites
by Emerian Rich

Makeup Tricks / Tips:

- ☠ NYX (not to be confused with NYC) shadows and powders
- ☠ Liquid black eyeliner art – don't be afraid to paint outside the lines
- ☠ Glitter plunger – to spray a favorite glitter onto wet eyeliner– instant glitter glue
- ☠ Prosthetic glue – to glitter up your eyes without worrying about it coming off
- ☠ Sparkle nail polish to add small dots on eyeliner dots – not directly on face and not too close to eye… that hurts!

Clothing Items:

- ☠ Stripey knee socks (black and white are kinda out, choose another color or go with a non-striped pattern)
- ☠ Wrist warmers or fingerless gloves
- ☠ Scarves – all different textures… but must be soft to the skin
- ☠ Layered, multi-textured skirts of all lengths
- ☠ "Emz has her own unique style. I've known some very fashion conscious people, but they're usually dressing to impress others. Emz dresses to express herself. I especially noticed the creativity of her eye make-up. The two sides were deliberately coordinated but not identical. They were unique—like Emz." ~H.E. Roulo

100 alt Fashion Styles

by Mimielle

This is a list of 100 fashion substyles. I want you to test your visualization skills to see how many you can call to mind. Alternative fashion is nothing new, although we like to pretend it is and that dressing artfully is a modern concept. Truthfully, it is centuries old and meant much the same then as it does now, a public visual statement outside mainstream culture for whatever reason. This list is not all-inclusive and leans heavily towards my biases and some I know you addicts have. Hopefully it will be entertaining and maybe give you a few new inspirations as well.

The Goths

1. TradGoth/Oldschool
2. CyberGoth
3. Romantic Goth
4. Nu-Goth/Soft Goth
5. Pastel Goth & Creepy Cute
6. Deathrocker
7. BabyBat
8. Rivet Head
9. BabyDoll Goth
10. Faerie Goth
11. ShiroGoth/White Goth
12. Corporate Goth
13. Victorian Goth
14. Hippie Goth
15. J-Goth
16. Military Goth
17. Tribal Goth
18. Geek Goth
19. Medieval Goth
20. Cabaret Goth
21. Carnival/Circus Goth
22. Casual Goth
23. Haute Goth
24. Glam Goth
25. Metal Head
26. Steampunk Goth
27. Perky Goth
28. Emo Goth
29. Vampire Goth
30. Mopey Goth
31. Festival Goth

The Lolitas

Not all of these are sub-sub-styles, more like classifications below the first three. But it is helpful to classify them in order to sort them out from each other. Plus I like them.

32. Gothic
33. Classic
34. Sweet
35. Punk
36. Kuro, Shiro, other single color
37. Princess/Hime
38. Guro
39. Aristocrat/Madam
40. Ouji/Kodona (Boystyle)
41. Dandy
42. Wa
43. Sailor
44. Qi
45. Country
46. Casual

The Punks & Anarchists

47. Old school Punk
48. Anarcho-Punk
49. Steampunk
50. Clockpunk
51. Dieselpunk
52. Teslapunk
53. Skatepunk

The Neos

54. Neo-Victorian
55. Neo-Roccoco
56. Neo-Romantic
57. Neo-Edwardian
58. Neo-Retro (1960's-70's reinventions)
59. Neo-Ludwig
60. Neo-Flapper/Gatsby

The Retros

61. Pinup
62. Rockabilly
63. Hippie
64. Bohemian
65. Disco
66. Indie
67. Mod
68. Hipster (many types, often a strange hybrid of retro and ultramodern)
69. T-Bird/Greaser
70. Zoot
71. Laid-Back 80's Miami Vice/Magnum

Japanese Street Styles

72. Visual Kei, Oshare Kei
73. Gyaru/Gyaru-o
74. Lolita* the sub-sub-styles listed above in their category.
75. Decora
76. Dolly Kei
77. Mori Girl (and Boy)
78. Cult Party Kei (CPK)
79. Yamamba, Manba, Ganguro (sub-style of Gyaru, a small resurgence of Ganguro is currently being seen in 2014)
80. Angura Kei & Shiro Nuri
81. Fairy Kei, Magical Girl styles (these styles are merging somewhat with the new Sailor Moon merchandising and upcoming 6 <3 Princess, including the Shu Uemura x Takashi Murakami collaboration here)

* The Scenesters*

I had to get another cup of coffee before even attempting to unravel a few for this one!

82. Glamcore
83. Screamo (see Grunge as well)
84. Hardcore
85. Pop Scene (overlap with Rave)
86. Hippie Scene
87. Bubblegum Scene (Oh Avril, you are here now)
88. Candy Genderchi
89. Emo (though there is debate whether this belongs here, it is a sub-style and very closely related.)

* The Unclasssified*

These are a thing, they just did not seem to fit well in any category and I am less familiar with them.

90. Chav (pre-Scene and current incarnation)
91. Chonga
92. Chola
93. HipHop
94. Industrial
95. Rave (Candy Rave has Scene crossover)
96. Emocore (ties to Goth and Emo itself)
97. Ero Kawaii (see Bubblegum Scene though both may not like the association)
98. Grunge (I am sure there are sub-sub-styles within but I will leave as an exercise for the readers to sort them.)
99. New Romanticism/Blitz kids (undergoing a slight bout of new popularity related to a small Synthpop revival but not quite full-blown retro)
100. Ethnic Fashion (and surrounding cultural appropriation controversies)

So, how many did you get a visual for? How many were interesting enough to look up? And finally the poll is below…what is YOUR style?

Whatever it is – Stay Beautiful, addicts!

back to black

by Mimielle

with art by Lnoir

How to create a stylishly dark wardrobe on a budget

Are the neons, pastel colors and eye-bending prints in recent fashion offerings disappointing you lately?

Do you prowl the mall with something different, something darker, in mind?

Does the idea of a monotone grey-to-black wardrobe appeal to you?

If so, I'm glad you found us here. A thrifty yet stylishly dark wardrobe is within reach of the imaginative and crafty. In the course of an afternoon spent at the thrift shops and then back home with the washing machine and some black Rit dye powder, you can create the wardrobe of your dreams.

As a bonus, you can freshen up the blacks in your wardrobe, give new life to your favorite faded black jeans or black shirts, and darken any lighter pieces you already have. Supplementing your basic wardrobe with inexpensive, thrifted items can leave you more cash for a coveted pair of shoes, accessories, hair dye, makeup, or other items that are not so easy to DIY! It's fun to be able to say you've dyed your own clothes to coordinate into your wardrobe and it is a creative and unique way to express yourself.

Once you've done a black load or two, branch out and explore the many possibilities for bleaching and dying. Dip-dye and ombre, dying custom canvas shoes, dyeing a canvas book bag or backpack, even branching out into room decor can inspire beautiful pieces. 'Plain' shirts and boring clothes hanging on the rack will never look the same to you again, and others will tempt you to re-create them!

So — to the project itself then!

Determine your budget for the project, and then take some time to make a list of items you'd like to add to your wardrobe. Keep an open mind to what you may find (on a whim?). A button-down shirt can be worn many ways, so can a cardigan. T-shirts are always a layering staple and are good basics to look for. On thrift-shopping day, wear an outfit and shoes easy to get in and out of or to try things on over because thrift shops don't always have dressing rooms. Try things on even if they aren't 'your size', I've found many thrifted items are miss-marked in size and actually fit or have been shrunk/stretched. Take your time and read the fabric content tags and buy items that contain at least 50% natural fiber content for best results. Cotton is always a safe bet and 50% cotton items are plentiful.

My experience is with Rit powder dye, in a top loading washing machine, with cotton as the basic fabric content, but I will refer you to the Rit Dye

Studio for everything from stovetop and bucket dying, to using a front loading machine or even your sink.

As always, parental permission and supervision are a good idea for dying projects if you aren't familiar with using a washing machine yet. Reserve the whole day for the dye project. It takes several hours from start to finish and cannot be rushed. You must also allow time to do your cleanup directly afterwards for your washer, dryer, sink, pot, etc., and any utensils used, in order to prevent staining.

The keys to successful dying at home are:

Fabric Choices: Natural fabrics will dye best and darkest, mixed fabrics will dye lighter, and synthetics including synthetic trim may not take dye well at all.

Using Enough Dye: For black, I double the recipe of the dye and the salt.

Weighing: Properly estimating the items to be dyed and using the correct load size and dye ratios, can be tricky. If you find quite a few great pieces or a jacket, you may need to do two dying sessions!

Follow the Directions Exactly: The Rit Studio lists all the methods and directions so everyone will find a method they can use successfully.

You will need:

1. A washing machine, non-reactive pot and stove, sink or bucket

2. Dye: powder or liquid. Refer to The Rit Studio site ritstudio.com for your method and YouTube videos for tips on dying things black.

3. Salt or vinegar as a fixative depending on your fabric content.

4. Liquid laundry detergent.

5. Old clothes to wear, gloves, old towels, paper towels, cleanup supplies.

6. (Optional but recommended) Rit Color Stay Dye Fixative.

Once you have successfully created a black wardrobe, be sure to tune in to HorrorAddicts.net for fashion news and ideas in each podcast and check my Monday a la Mode posts on the blog featuring Look Books, Mood Boards, how-to's and fashion tips. You can always find more information on my HorrorAddicts.net projects at Mimielle.Net. Soon we shall be taking the shears to our newly dyed creations to transform them even further!

Until then, Stay Beautiful, addicts.

<3 Mimielle

Costume blunders to avoid

by Emerian Rich

Costuming is all about being prepared. Here are some tips from our costume blunders over the years.

☠ If you are going to cover yourself with liquid latex, shave any hair in the area and have all other hair tied up and protected. Very painful trying to get it off later.

☠ Never leave home without touch-up makeup. Nothing worse than being at a party and realizing your makeup is messed up half-way through with nothing to fix it with.

☠ To avoid nip slip, wear a nude strapless bra and underwear under mummy bandages. The bandages WILL slip. Don't let yourself become the victim of this costume's faults.

☠ If you are going to wear prosthetics, eat BEFORE you go to the party. A lot of these attachables make it hard to enjoy food and drink.

☠ Horns that are supposed to be applied with adhesive, should be applied with adhesive. I once used the squeezable horn to "suction" it on my forehead and after 8 hours of work, the "sucking" process had created real horns on my forehead out of my own skin and blood. It sounds cool, it isn't. Incredibly painful.

☠ If you are going as Bride of Frankenstein, use a base or fake hair to help construct the hair tower so that you don't have to tease all of your hair. Painful to brush out later.

☠ It's always better to make costumes from real clothes and makeup rather than polyester

243

costumes and greasy clown makeup. Do your best with what you have, it will appear more authentic. Halloween stores are great for accessories like striped socks, hair attachments, or jewelry.

10 Costume Cheats

by Mimielle

1. Black eyeliner as black lipstick. Outline your lips with a sharpened point, then fill in.

2. Thin pieces of torn toilet paper/facial tissue and eyeliner glue applied in layers to make scars or burns or other FX instead of using liquid latex, spirit gum, or liquid collodian. Newspaper-stuffed bustles. Stuff newspaper or tissue paper into Walmart bags, secure under bustle poufs and get ready for a rustle in that bustle.

3. Glue a bag of $1 spider rings (cut off ring part first) all over a thrift store white nightgown draped with bagged spiderwebs. Rub dark eyeliner under eyes and a bit on lips for an instant creepy lady costume.

4. Use Baby Powder to set the lightest cheap cream drugstore foundation, it will pale it out quite a bit.

5. Cut and shape craft feathers to use in place of expensive exotic large false eyelashes.

6. Craft glitter manicure: Paint nails with desired color, let dry. Then paint with clear, dip in craft glitter, let dry, repeat, then seal with more clear. (NOTE: do not use craft glitter near eyes for any reason.)

7. Steal, erm I mean borrow your friend's fast food uniform and be that for Halloween.

8. Paint your face with a Dia de los Muertos design and borrow or thrift an old wedding dress and veil.

9. Wear a thrifted or borrowed black suit and tie, with a   full-head white stocking cap and white gloves and go as Slenderman. ♀

245

Horror Survival Guide

nightshade on survival

In this section you'll find some good advice on survival. We can all benefit from advice sometimes, especially when it comes from other horror addicts. Although I must admit I'm a little bit disappointed that there was not a section on how to know if your boyfriend is really a vampire. You see, vampires can be sneaky and I think it's important to know if someone close to you is really a vampire. Here are a few ways to tell if your boyfriend is a vampire:

- ☠ If he never drinks wine or just likes to say the phrase, "I never drink...wine," he may be a vampire.
- ☠ If he smells like burnt bacon when you go to the beach, he may be a vampire.
- ☠ If he hisses like an angry cat when he sees a church, he may be a vampire.
- ☠ If you cut yourself, nothing comes out, and he says, "That's weird," he may be a vampire.
- ☠ If he wants to take you shopping for a new casket and keeps saying, "This looks really comfortable," he may be a vampire.

There you have it addicts. Remember to watch for the signs and if you do want to date a vampire, make sure you always wear a turtle-neck sweater. Too much neck skin can make the evening end quite abruptly.

Surviving Zombies

by Jessica Robinson

I am obsessed with zombies, and I have been since the first time I saw *Night of the Living Dead*. Not a day goes by that I don't think about zombies and what I need to do to survive the uprising—if and when it occurs. If zombie books and movies have taught me anything, it's that the zombie apocalypse will happen swiftly and catch the vast majority of us unprepared. I don't plan on getting caught in that trap, and neither should you. I follow a few simple rules to make sure I'm ready for what the future may bring.

1. Have a plan.

Are you going to stay in your home and defend what's yours or are you going to make a break for a safe place? Where is that safe place going to be? How are you going to get there? If you're staying in your home, do you have a way to fortify it?

This topic has been discussed in my household on numerous occasions, and we decided we would much rather take our chances in the wild rather than in the city. Thankfully, we live close to the highway and have 4-wheel drive vehicles, so our escape plan is to head for the mountains. The terrain up there is difficult for zombies to traverse, and it's far enough away from their food source (people) that we'll be safe. With a few supplies and wilderness survival skills, our goal is to avoid zombies at all costs.

We have also discussed staying in the house should the opportunity to escape not arise. My plan is to turn the attic into a safe house full of supplies (food and water) and weapons. There will be one ladder inside the house to access the room, along with an escape hatch/sniper window cut into the roof. The house itself isn't that secure with all of its windows and doors, and books and films have shown boarded windows don't really stop zombies on the hunt anyway. However, most of them can't climb, so getting to higher ground is a good idea. And if they can climb, we'll make sure to pull the ladder up after us.

No matter what route you choose to stay safe from the zombies, always, *always* make sure you have another escape route. The best defense against zombies is avoidance.

2. Know your surroundings.

Since no one knows when or where the zombies will rise and attack, it's important to always know your surroundings. No matter where you are, make sure you know where the exits are. Be aware of how many people around you could become potential threats. Take note of objects that could be used as weapons should you have to fight your way out.

When I go to the gym, work, the store, wherever, I take a few moments to survey my surroundings. I try to stay aware of where exits are and how long it will take me to get to one. I make a mental note of how many people are around and the best way to avoid them when it's time to escape. If escape is impossible, I look for a good place to hide that's out of the way until the panic dies down. I also look for things that could be turned into weapons. If there isn't anything that would make a good weapon, then I will search for something that will keep a safe distance between me and the zombie so I can escape. For example, this could be a chair or a long pole to keep the zombies away. These are only intended to be temporary solutions so that I can get to safety.

Knowing these things could mean the difference between life and death.

After the zombies rise, don't ever go into a place that you have no way of getting out of. This is guaranteeing death or infection. And always be aware of what is going on around you. That means traveling in pairs (at least) could be beneficial. You have a lookout if you need it. Your life is too important to take unnecessary risks.

3. Have supplies on hand.

There will still be supplies floating around in the world once zombies take over, but getting them may prove challenging. If you have a stockpile, that makes things much easier in the long run and gives you time before needing to run out and get more. Again, avoiding zombies as much as possible increases your chance of survival.

4. Have multiple weapons and know how to use them effectively.

While we all want to have a gun around to fight off zombies, they may not always be the best weapon for the job. They are loud and only work with the proper ammunition. Now, I'm not saying get rid of them all together. No, no, no. They are still your best defense. They allow distance between you and your intended target, and they are the most effective way of killing the undead.

However, know *how* to use them, know when to use them, have various kinds (handguns, rifles, etc.), and make sure to have plenty of ammo. If you can, learn how to reload your own ammo. This will save you from having to raid stores for more. Also, being proficient with your weapon—knowing how to aim and fire it—will minimize wasting ammo. If possible, carry one with you at all times and within the applicable laws of where you live. Again, you never know when/where zombies will rise. Make sure you can protect yourself and loved ones.

In addition, it's important to have silent weapons that are effective at killing. These could include katanas or machetes, but make sure you know how to use them. You don't want to end up hurting yourself or others while battling zombies. And make sure they are sharp. They have to be quick and effective at taking your opponents head off—especially if you have to be that close to do it.

5. Make sure you have access to a clean water source.

This is probably *the most important item* on this list. *You can only survive for three days without water.* Water also carries a lot of pathogens, so you need to make sure your source is clean or you have the ability to make it clean. You cannot fight the undead if you're doubled over in pain or vomiting every few minutes. Thankfully, boiling water is a good way to make it safe, but there are also water bottles and purification systems that can be used to make water potable. Make these part of your supply stash, along with bottled water.

Once the dead rise, the world will be thrown into chaos. But with a little planning and foresight, you don't have to become a victim. Taking the time now to prepare for zombies will give you a better chance of survival when they rise. If books and movies have taught us anything else, it's that humans will need every advantage we can get.

hoRRoR addicts Guide to cats

by Sumiko Saulson

As a horror aficionado, you have probably encountered your fair share of gruesome and grizzly tales involving rabid dogs like *Cujo*, wolves of both the natural and the preternatural kind, and even birds, ala Alfred Hitchcock. In all of these encounters with the horrific creatures of your nightmares, I imagine it never occurred to you that you should have to fear your sweet little furball Fluffy.

Well, I am here to warn you otherwise.

Here are the some things every horror addict should do in order to prevent an all out feline rebellion in your home.

Never bring your cat back from the dead

Stephen King (in *Pet Sematary*, 1983) and Edgar Allen Poe (in *The Black Cat*, 1843) have issued warnings against this whole idea of cat necromancy. Sure, it seems like a good idea at first. We've all heard that cats have nine lives, so why not resurrect them? It's only natural, right?

Unfortunately, as the doomed owners of Church and Pluto can attest, this is never a good idea. First of all, they never come back the same. Take Pluto, for example. Sure, he had every right to be a bit prickly towards his owner. After all, it was his owner who killed him. That was no excuse for the unadulterated rage and need for revenge, though, now was it?

In the case of Louis Creed's cat, Winston Churchill (aka Church), he wasn't even responsible for the cat's death, but it still came back in a foul mood with a funky odor.

Second of all, one or more of your family members will die as a result of your cat resurrection. Even if you don't like your wife or child all that much, it's still not worth it. The cat might alert the authorities and before you know it, you're off to the gallows.

If your cat starts hissing, don't go kissing

Alternately known as: "When your cat starts hating, don't start dating"

Sleepwalkers (Stephen King) and both the 1942 and the 1982 versions of *Cat People* warn us that if your cat starts freaking out at the sight of your new beau, he or she is probably some kind of supernatural human-eating pseudo-feline hybrid monster who wants to kill and eat you.

Never kill a cat lady

The Uncanny (1977) consists of three vignettes, two of which illustrate the fact that feline vengeance is not always self-centered. Cats can and will protect their duly appointed cat-lady. Whether it is a crazy old woman who dies and leaves her home to a houseful of apparently unaltered madly breeding housecats, or the wife with a loyal feline ally, these cats can and will avenge their beloved human. No, it's not just the rats' love for Willard you have to worry about.

The third of the vignette demonstrates that love is a two way street. Never mess with the pet of a poor little orphan girl, especially if that girl is a budding witch.

This also applies to cat men, who we like to refer to as "cat lads."

Alternately, there are ladies who actually ARE cats (see *Cat People* above).

You don't want to mess with them, either.

horror addicts guide to Good health

by Sparky Lee Anderson

Being a horror addict means you spend countless hours sitting and watching a television/computer screen, or lying down while you read the latest zombie novel. Either way, when you're a horror nerd, I doubt I'll find you outside at seven a.m. going for a jog. We are a night breed, we adhere to our odd sleeping hours and viewing practices with a tenacious grip, unwilling to apologize and unwilling to change. Being a horror fan is not just a hobby, it's a way of life. That being said, horror fans can often be out of shape. We're not like sports fans. We don't toss the pig skin around or shoot hoops for fun. We sit in groups and discuss film and the written word with egregious sarcasm and impeccable wit. The only exercise in our discussions are dramatic hand gestures and the lifting and falling of our cups of java and/or alcoholic beverage. We are often pale faced, sleep deprived and tragically pessimistic. I have compiled an inventory of useful information in an effort to demonstrate how to stay in optimal health as a horror addict.

Sleep:

One common thing we horror addicts frequently suffer from is a lack of sleep. Not getting enough sleep over a period of days or weeks can cause serious issues with one's mental stability. You want to ensure you're getting the proper eight or nine hours a night to stay fresh, alert, and sane. When the shit hits the fan, if you're snoozing, you're dead. Try stocking up on caffeine pills and energy drinks just to keep in your personal stash in case anything goes down and you're too sleepy to fight it or much less care.

Because we often stay up late at night, sleeping later during the day, we often suffer from the lack of sunshine. This leads to a pale-faced and tired horror addict. I recommend taking vitamin D on a daily basis, it's referred to as the "sunshine vitamin" so this can help combat some of the fatigue from staying up all night. Mix in a nice B vitamin complex and you'll have a little pep in your step for when the zombies come. You don't want to be caught with your immune system down in the event of a zombie apocalypse—or when you're running from a serial killer—so ensuring you have proper nutrition and are getting your daily doses of vitamins and minerals is essential to a healthy survivor.

Dental Care:

Dental Care is important. In the event you unwittingly become one of the walking dead, you'll want to ensure you have a set of strong healthy teeth. You'll need them to tear flesh off of bone and for breaking through skulls to reach the prized brains. A healthy set of regularly flossed chompers could mean the difference between a well fed zombie and one that can't keep up with the others, ultimately becoming a joke amongst the zombie masses. No one's afraid of a toothless zombie.

Diet:

In the spirit of eating, I also recommend you eat smaller meals, more frequently throughout the day, rather than one large heavy meal once or twice a day. This can really slow your digestion system, making you tired and feeling bloated. You'll be of no use during a plague of the undead, if you're stuck on the toilet for hours. Keep your diet clean, with lots of fresh fruits and vegetables. Also, eat lots of fiber to ensure you have a healthy digestion system, and to help with weight management. If you can't run, you'll never get away from the vampires. It's my understanding that they're quite fast and if you're a round, slow, and constipated, you'll be a prime target for zombies, vampires, werewolves, and serial killers. It's also important to stay hydrated at all times. Stock up on clean drinking water to keep your body fresh, flushed out, and energized. While you're stocking yourself up on fresh water and vegetables, be sure to swing by the fresh herbs aisle at your local grocery store, and grab a few dozen bulbs of garlic too. Seriously people, it's cheap, there's no excuse to NOT have garlic in your home at all times.

Physical Health:

You want to ensure you are partaking in a regular cardio and weight lifting regime. When you're running for your life, you need endurance and strength. A simple routine of daily running or jogging in conjunction with some muscle resistance exercises, can make the difference of you out-running a psychopath or zombie. If you're a heavy smoker with no muscle mass, barely able to breathe or catch your breath, coughing the entire way, you're going to fall victim to your pursuer. Ladies, work on your core and upper body strength, weapons are not light and you'll need to be able to carry and utilize your own without the help of someone else. You'll need a strong body inside and out to make it in the harsh world of the horror addict. Yoga is great for learning proper breathing techniques, relaxing your breath, and strengthening and lengthening your muscles. You'll be a lean, mean fighting machine when the shit hits the fan, and a worthy adversary to anyone/anything that may cross your path.

Vaccinations and Inoculations:

There are a multitude of mysterious illnesses that the W.H.O (World Health Organization) have created questionably successful vaccines for. I guess it's better to be safe than sorry and make sure you're up to date on all your inoculations and boosters. It wouldn't be very plausible, in a frightful situation, to end up dying from a tetanus infection. Most serious plagues result from communicable illnesses. See the film *Outbreak (1995)* for further explanation. The flip side of vaccines is that if the powers that be decide to thin the herd out a little, then vaccines would be the way to do it. Use your own discretion, but definitely get your tetanus shot.

Spiritual Health:

Keep the faith alive. It's easy to become a "Negative Nelly" during an apocalypse situation. There's no food, everything's dirty, and you can't find toilet paper. It's important that we as horror addicts keep our spirits up. A strong sense of faith can go a long way. It can also be a great weapon against demons and poltergeists. It's important to believe in something bigger than ourselves. It can provide great comfort on those nights that you're too afraid to sleep, or when you require some extra spiritual protection. Try hanging a few crucifixes in your home for some added protection. In a world where "Good versus Evil" occurs on a regular basis, it's helpful to have the "Big Guy" on your side with two enthusiastic thumbs up in your favor. We've all seen how something as simple as reciting the Lord's Prayer or saying Jesus' name can drive evil demons out from one's home and/or loved ones.

Develop a Strong Posse:

Whether you're suffering from a series of intense horror nightmares resulting in a lack of sleep and complete mental breakdown, or if you find yourself in an apocalyptic situation, you will need a series of connections that will undoubtedly save your ass. I have developed a system for picking my friends over the years as my horror addiction grew and developed in to its own entity. I have some guidelines for people that you will need to know:

The Smart One: You'll need one really smart friend. This will be the individual that figures out how to purify water, where to sleep, make booby traps, and explain what you're up against in laymen's terms.

The Tough Guy: You'll need one fearless individual on your team. This will be the person that scouts for new locations, runs up against monsters of ANY persuasion, and throws the first punch at the bad guy. This will keep you safe and relatively clean.

The Reasonable One: This will be the person that keeps the tough guy from going off half-cocked, ultimately making your situation even worse. They will also keep you from eating things that could be tainted and/or poisonous.

The Mother/Father Figure: This person will keep you grounded and make you dig deep for confidence and fearlessness. They will remind you where you're from and who you really are. Frightful circumstances can break even the strongest of minds, the mother/father figure will keep you strong and confident while reminding you what you are fighting for.

The Attractive One: There should just be something nice to look at in a world full of evil, carnage, and despair. This person will make you reach deep inside yourself and comb your matted hair and wash your dirty face even though the shit is hitting the fan and there are more important things to worry about.

The Anal One: All teams need one uptight, anally retentive individual. This person can sometimes keep you on track in a detail oriented fashion. They can tally in their head, which is helpful because you may not have pen and paper while running from an ax-wielding psychopath.

The Ex-military Guy: This guy is ready to fight and has extensive weapons knowledge. He's gone through basic training so you know he's tough. He can often be found with the *tough guy*.

The Nurse/EMT or LPN: Every group needs at least one health professional. Someone who knows how to treat wounds, stop the spread of an infection, or successfully amputate a limb if need be. This personal knows where all the antibiotics of the world are located and can administer life-saving techniques without breaking a sweat.

The Smart Ass: The smart ass will keep your spirits and morale up by cracking inappropriate jokes at dire times. During periods of quiet, they can provide endless entertainment. The sad thing about this is that, the smart ass usually dies early in any given horror scenario. We will miss you smart ass.

I have demonstrated the importance of being a healthy horror addict so you can handle any horrifying situation you may encounter. We know through film and books, how dreadful our world can be and how quickly things can take a turn for the worse. It's crucial to be prepared both mentally and physically for any appalling direction our world might take. Evil can transpire at any given time. Be prepared.

Stay Healthy, Stay Strong,

Sparky ☠

pRacTicinG Safe SatisfacTion

by Laurel Anne Hill

It can happen to you at any time, the need for a horror fix. Maybe you're enjoying an overcooked Big Mac and realize your tongue searches in vain for the taste of blood. Or maybe you're giving an important presentation at work. You find yourself scanning your audience for a satisfying pair of dark, brooding eyes, but everyone's sneaking a peek at their cell phones. Perhaps you and your significant other cuddle together to view a romantic movie at night, when you'd rather download a *Nightmare with Freddy* feature.

How can you satisfy your horror cravings without losing your cool, your job or that special person in your life?

Caffeine, chocolate or gum might provide a momentary diversion, at least until you can mellow out with a cigarette or glass of wine. Even alcohol or a smoke—if those indulgences comprise part of your lifestyle—won't help for long, at least, not without backup. And forget the thought of hard drugs. Isn't one major addiction—horror—problem enough? Besides, when you need to read about a vampire's midnight snack, hear a zombie munch on Kentucky Fried Brains, or see Mr. Horrible peeling the skin off of some damsel in distress like the gal is a human potato, only a dose of horror media will satisfy.

So how can you cope when thwarted?

The next time horror-deprivation ignites your flames of anxiety in horror-adverse surroundings, reach for your personal portable anxiety-extinguishing device: your imagination.

For example:

1. Need to taste that handsome vampire's blood? Bite the inside of your cheek. Use your imagination.

2. Giving that powerful presentation at work? Forget your hunger to see dark, brooding eyes in your audience. Pretend that the alien cell phones in the room will soon suck out their owners' eyeballs.

3. Does that romantic movie give you indigestion? Focus on the wall behind your flat screen. Flesh-eating mutant cockroaches could crawl out of a crevice at any moment.

The above-listed advice should help you achieve a more manageable state of mind and allow your crisis to recede. Use of the imagination helps horror addicts practice "safe satisfaction" until they can return to the book, movie, podcast, graphic novel, or videogame of their desire.

horror addicts almanac

OCTOBER

October for horror addicts is a month of excitement, anticipation, and stress. Prepare yourself, get lots of sleep in the months preceding so that you are rested and raring to go. When the clock strikes orange, you want to have your energy at its max. During the month, be sure to keep your strength up by taking black cat naps, drinking a lot of water, and eating well. Skipping meals will just turn you into a raving bloody lunatic... which might be fun for others to point and laugh at, but it won't be helpful for finishing your costume on time.

HORRORSCOPE: JACK-O-LANTERN

People born in October are like Jack-o-lantern's. They shine bright on the inside, but sometimes don't show others the light they have inside until they are close enough to get burned. Don't camouflage your bright light with a crooked smile, but do be wary of overenthusiastic fans who will take a chunk out of you.

To Do List:

☐   1. Create at least one costume.

☐   2. Share candy and sweets.

☐   3. Watch your favorite horror flix.

☐   4. Listen to spooky tunes.

☐   5. Shop for home decor.

☐   6. Honor your deceased relatives/friends.

MOVIE LIST

Pretty much any horror movie is a go this month.

Halloween movies

Hocus Pocus, 1993

Sleepy Hollow, 1999

Trick 'r Treat, 2007

Halloweentown movies

Night of the Demons, 1988

TRIVIA

- National Blood Donor Month
- Count Chocula cereal first sold in October, 1971 and comes out every fall.
- Last Friday of Oct: Frankenstein Friday
- Oct 30th Mischief Night also known as Hell Night, Trick Night, Gate Night, Devil's Night.

HORROR DATES TO REMEMBER

1. James Whitmore, *Them!* 1954
2. *The Twilight Zone* launches, 1959
3. Neve Campbell, *Scream* 1996
4. Anne Rice, author
5. Clive Barker, author
6. Jeremy Sisto, *May* 2002
7. Dylan Baker, *Trick r Treat* 2007
8. Sigourney Weaver, *Ghostbusters* 1984
9. Guillermo del Toro, dir., *Hellboy* 2004
10. Ed D. Wood, Jr., dir., *Night of the Ghouls* 1959
11. Stephen Moyer, *True Blood* 00's TV
12. Dorothy K. Haynes, author
13. Chris Carter, screenwriter, *Millennium* 90's TV
14. Udo Kier, *Blade* 1998
15. The "From Hell" letter postmarked by Jack the Ripper to investigators, 1888
16. Oscar Wilde, author of *The Picture of Dorian Gray*
17. Julie Adams, *Creature from the Black Lagoon* 1954
18. Klaus Kinski, *Nosferatu the Vampyre* 1979
19. John Lithgow, *Raising Cain* 1992
20. Bela Lugosi, *Dracula* 1931
21. Everett McGill, *Twin Peaks* 90's TV
22. Christopher Lloyd, *The Addams Family* 1991
23. Sam Raimi, writer & dir., *The Evil Dead*, 1981
24. John Kassir, voice of the Crypt Keeper
25. Victoria Frances, artist
26. Dziady, a slavic celebration to honor ancestors by feasting at the graveyard.
27. Channon Roe, *Kindred: The Embraced* 90's TV
28. Joe R. Lansdale, author
29. Winona Ryder, *Beetlejuice* 1988
30. *The War of the Worlds* airs on radio, 1938
31. Halloween

NOVEMBER

November is a time of recovery for the horror addict. Most of us hibernate and incorporate hoodies into our wardrobe, hoody up. It's also a time for illness to creep up because we've neglected our bodies' needs for rest and proper nutrition in the stress and drama of Halloween. Stock up on cold deterrents and Vitamin C. Sleep and rest as much as you can. Indulge in comfort foods to gain back some of the nutrients starved out of your system. Allow yourself some in-bed reading or on-couch movie watching days. Take short, easy walks to build up your endurance.

HORRORSCOPE: ZOMBIE

Horror addicts born in November truly are zombies this month. Although you may feel low on brains, don't worry, a few months of after-Halloween recovery will get you back on track. Until then, don't travel alone and be wary of rednecks carrying shotguns.

To Do List
☐ 1. Go shopping! After Halloween sales start early!
☐ 2. Properly stow away your Halloween decor and costumes that aren't left out all year.
☐ 3. Sleep.
☐ 4. Spend time with friends and family that you neglected during the busy season.
☐ 5. Scrapbook or journal about your fab October.
☐ 6. Give thanks for all we take for granted. Black eyeliner, freedom to watch horror, and after Halloween sales.

MOVIE LIST

Thankskilling, 2009

Addams Family Values, 1993

Home Sweet Home, 2013

All Souls Day, 2005

Blood Freak, 1972

Grindhouse, 2007

TRIVIA

- ☠ National Novel Writing Month
- ☠ Nov. 2nd, Dia De Los Muertos
- ☠ Nov. 2nd, All Souls Day
- ☠ Nov. 5th, Guy Fawkes Day, Bonfire Night
- ☠ Nov. 15th, First mothman sighting

HORROR DATES TO REMEMBER

1. Edward Van Sloan, "Van Helsing", *Dracula* 1931
2. *Jacob's Ladder* released 1990
3. Tom Savini, horror icon of gore effects
4. Martin Balsam, *Psycho* 1960
5. Robert Patrick, *Terminator 2* 1991
6. Thandie Newton, *Interview with the Vampire* 1994
7. Myra Jones, body double for Janet Leigh in *Psycho* 1960
8. Abraham "Bram" Stoker, author
9. *Silent Night, Deadly Night* released 1984
10. Neil Gaiman, author
11. Bill Moseley, *Night of the Living Dead* 1990
12. Jacques Tourneur, dir. *I Walked with a Zombie* 1943
13. Robert Lewis Stevenson, author, S*trange Case of Dr. Jekyll and Mr. Hyde*
14. Veronica Lake, *I Married a Witch* 1942
15. Sydney Tamiia Poitier, *Death Proof* 2007
16. *A Nightmare on Elm Street* released 1984
17. Martin Scorsese, dir. *Shutter Island* 2010
18. Peta Wilson, *The League of Extraordinary Gentlemen* 2003
19. Nigel Bennett, Lacroix in *Forever Knight* 90's TV
20. Bo Derek, *Horror 101* 2001
21. Lindsey Haun, *Village of the Damned* 1995
22. Jamie Lee Curtis, *Halloween* 1978
23. Boris Karloff, horror icon
24. Garrett Dillahunt, *The Last House on the Left* 2009
25. Katie Cassidy, *Black Christmas* 2006
26. Kristin Bauer van Straten, *True Blood* 00's TV
27. First appearance of Count von Count on *Sesame Street* 1972
28. Ryan Kwanten, *Dead Silence* 2007
29. Lucas Black, *American Gothic* 90's TV
30. Henry Selick, dir. *The Nightmare Before Christmas* 1993

DECEMBER

For horror addicts, December can be a mixed bag. Although you are recovering slowly from Halloween activities, you are often asked to participate in family events and feel obligated to shop for everyone else's favorite holiday. Relentless nagging and family feuds can make this month the wrong kind of horror story. The positive horror addict will remember this is a chance to don your horror tree with *Nightmare Before Christmas* ornaments and wrap gifts in black paper. After all, gifts might mean you'll get that horror box set you've been lusting after!

HORRORSCOPE: SKELETON

Horror addicts born in December often feel stripped to the bone by others, but don't be scared to stand up for yourself. So what if other's like to keep you locked in their closets? Let yourself be heard by rattling those bones.

To Do List
☐   1. Celebrate Humbug Day by wearing a black Santa hat.
☐   2. Prepare your survival kit. Whether it be natural disaster, zombie apocalypse, or un-happy sister-in-law attack, you'll be good to go.
☐   3. Detox from Christmas Carole overload by listening to horror tunes.
☐   4. Keep antacid on hand for overeating and over-familying.
☐   5. Kidnap Mr. Sandy Claws.
☐   6. Read some haunted horror.

MOVIE LIST

Silent Bloody Night, 1972
Black Christmas, 1974
Santa's Slay, 2005
Christmas Evil, 1980

Jack Frost, 1997
Santa Claws, 1996
Satan Claus, 1996
Wind Chill, 2007

TRIVIA

☠   Dec. 5th, Krampusnacht is celebrated in Alpine countries. This is the date where the Christmas demon Krampus comes and takes away naughty children.

☠   Dec. 21st Humbug Day

☠   Dec. 25th National Pumpkin Pie Day

HORROR DATES TO REMEMBER

1. Better Midler, *Hocus Pocus*, 1993
2. Johnathan Frid, Barnabas Collins on *Dark Shadows* 60's TV
3. Ozzy Osbourne
4. Tony Todd, director, *Candyman*, 1992
5. Walt Disney, creator of our childhood villains!
6. Patrick Bauchau, "Archon" in *Kindred: The Embraced*, 90's TV
7. Emily Browning, *Ghost Ship*, 2002
8. Ian Somerhalder, *TheVampire Diaries*, 00's TV
9. John Malkovich, *Shadow of the Vampire*, 2000
10. Lacy Fisher, *Chemical Peel*, 2014
11. Zienia Merton, Hammer House of M&S, 1984
12. Jennifer Connelly, *Dark City*, 1998
13. Wendie Malick, *Tales from the Crypt*, 90's TV
14. Ted Raimi, *The Evil Dead*, 1981
15. Stuart Townsend, *Queen of the Damned*, 2002
16. *Night Gallery* airs, 1970
17. Milla Jovovich, *Resident Evil*, 2002
18. Kaori Yuki, manga artist of *Godchild*
19. Nancy Kyes, *Halloween*, 1978
20. Jenny Agutter, *An American Werewolf in London*, 1981
21. Kiefer Sutherland, *The Lost Boys*, 1987
22. Freddie Francis, dir. *Son of Dracula*, 1974
23. Corey Haim, *The Lost Boys*, 1987
24. According to Russian folklore, a child born on this day will become a werewolf.
25. Rod Serling, *Twilight Zone*, 50's TV
26. *The Exorcist* released, 1973
27. Heather O'Rourke, *Poltergeist*, 1982
28. F. W. Murnau, director, Nosferatu, 1922
29. Dave McKean, goth artist
30. S. P. Somtow, writer, *Vampire Junction*
31. Anthony Hopkins, *Silence of the Lambs*, 1991

JANUARY

January for the Horror Addict can be depressing. You've recovered from Halloween officially, been traumatized by holiday family gatherings and gift giving, but while everyone else is ringing in a new year, you're just thinking about the ten months you still have to wait before you can be accepted for who you are by the general public. Carry on dark children, we shall have our day again and for now, why not host your own horror movie night. Your horror kin need some comfort too.

HORRORSCOPE: BLACK CAT

HorrorAddicts born in January should remember, you only have 9 lives, not 32. Take it easy sometimes. Even sly masterminds need a break every once in awhile. Others may think you're bad luck, but they are blaming you for their own faults. Sneaking around the place can keep you out of trouble, but if someone gets too close, don't be afraid to arch your back and hiss. Stay strong and pounce with pride.

Horror Addict New Year's Resolutions
☐   1. Watch more horror.
☐   2. Read more horror.
☐   3. Listen to spookier music.
☐   4. See more horror art.
☐   5. Donate blood.
☐   6. Host a movie night

MOVIE LIST

Terror Train, 1980
The Thing, 1982
Black Cat, 1934

Bloody New Year, 1987
Perfect Creature, 2006
Night Creature, 1978

TRIVIA

☠   National Blood Donor Month

☠   Jan 3rd Memento mori, a holiday in ancient
Rome where you acknowledge that you will die some day.

☠   Jan 19th, National Popcorn Day

☠   Jan 30th Chytroi, the third day of the Athenian
Anthesteria fest, devoted to expelling unwanted ghosts.

☠   Jan 31st Me-Dam-Me-Phi, a festival in Assam
which features offerings to departed ancestors.

HORROR DATES TO REMEMBER

1. James O'Barr, creator of *The Crow* comics
2. Louis Daguerre took the first photo of the moon, 1839
3. Jewel Shepard, Scream Queen
4. Jacob Grimm, co-author of Grimm's fairy tales
5. Marilyn Manson
6. Norman Reedus, Daryl, *The Walking Dead*, 00's TV
7. Charles Addams creator of *The Addams Family* 60's TV
8. David Bowie, *The Hunger*, 1983
9. Nina Dobrev, *The Vampire Diaries*, 00's TV
10. Trini Alvarado, *The Frighteners*, 1996
11. Felix Silla, Cousin Itt on *The Addams Family*, 60's TV
12. Rob Zombie
13. January 13th productions – A Little Night Fright 2007
14. Richard Laymon, author
15. Chad Lowe, Highway to Hell, 1991
16. John Carpenter, dir. *Halloween*, 1978
17. Eartha Kitt the original Catwoman
18. John Boorman, dir. *Exorcist II: The Heretic*, 1977
19. Edgar Allen Poe
20. Ken Page, *The Nightmare Before Christmas,* 1993
21. Geena Davis, *Beetlejuice*, 1988
22. Linda Blair, *The Exorcist*, 1973
23. Rutger Hauer, Anne Rice's original vision to play Lestat
24. Matthew Lillard, *Thir13en Ghosts*, 2001
25. Tobe Hooper, dir. *Salem's Lot*, 1979
26. Cameron Bright, *Night Visions*, 00's TV
27. Bridget Fonda, *Army of Darkness*, 1992
28. The Shining novel was released, 1977
29. Sam Trammell, *True Blood*, 00's TV
30. *Silence of the Lambs* released, 1991
31. Philip Glass, composer

FEBRUARY

February can be quite fun for the Horror Addict in love. What a wonderful time of year to celebrate your Morticia-Gomez love affair! For those less lucky in love, February doesn't have to be a downer. Lovely Valentine's massacre movies and biological heart Jello molds can make this month almost as special as our haunted holiday. For the fashion conscious, stock up on your reds this month. From deep blood red to shocking vibrant red, stores favor you this month.

HORRORSCOPE: DEMON

You've been told to go to Hell, but you've already been there. Embrace your sinister side and don some red latex. It's time to show everyone who's boss. Remember when on the prowl, watch out for chalk outlines and never give your name. Demon's can't be too careful who they allow to call them in the future. Don't become shackled by a one night release.

To Do List

☐ 1. Infuse your black wardrobe with bright red or crimson

☐ 2. Make a biological heart jello mold

☐ 3. Buy naughty gifts for your Morticia/Gomez

☐ 4. Celebrate villains on the 26th, Fairytale Day.

☐ 5. Watch presidential horror.

☐ 6. Don your finest Mardi Gras costume.

MOVIE LIST

Valentine, 2001
My Bloody Valentine, 1981
My Bloody Valentine, 2009
Candyman:
 Farewell to Flesh, 1995

The Tripper, 2006
Washingtonians, 2007
Abraham Lincoln:
 Vampire Killer, 2012
President's Day, 2010

TRIVIA

☠   National Organ Donor Month

☠   The *Sleepy Hollow* TV Series states George Washington was brought back as a zombie.

☠   A cat named Demon Cat has been haunting government buildings in Washington, D.C. for decades. Some believe he predicts assassinations.

☠   Abraham Lincoln's son, Willie Lincoln, is said to haunt the White House.

☠   Mobsters were killed in the St. Valentine's Day massacre in 1929, and at least one haunted Capone till his death.

HORROR DATES TO REMEMBER

1. Brandon Lee, *The Crow*, 1994
2. Duane Jones, Night of the Living Dead
3. Johnny Cannizzaro, *Dark Fantasy*, 2005
4. George A. Romero, dir. *Dawn of the Dead*, 1978
5. H. R. Giger, horror artist
6. Alice Eve, The Raven
7. Charles Dickens, author
8. Seth Green, *Buffy the Vampire Slayer* 00's TV
9. Frank Frazetta, illustrator "Vamperella" / Amy Lowell horror poet
10. Lon Chaney, Jr.
11. Leslie Nelson
12. Christina Ricci, *Sleepy Hollow*, 1999
13. Oliver Reed, *The Pit and the Pendulum*, 1991
14. Simon Pegg, *Shaun of the Dead*, 2004
15. *Fog Island* released 1945
16. Lisa Loring, Wednesday Addams, 60's TV
17. Don Coscarelli, dir. *Phantasm*, 1979
18. Jack Palance, *Bram Stoker's Dracula*, 1974
19. Laurell K. Hamilton, author
20. Richard Matheson, author
21. Jennifer Love Hewitt, *Ghost Whisperer*, 00's TV
22. Edward Gorey, artist
23. Terence Fisher, dir. *Horror of Dracula*, 1958
24. *Frostbitten* released in Sweden 2006
25. John Saul, author
26. James Wan, dir. *Saw*, 2004
27. Kate Mara, *American Horror Story*, 00's TV
28. Ali Larter, *House on Haunted Hill*, 1999

MARCH

Spring conjures thoughts of flowers and bunnies, but for the Horror Addict, this is the time to clean out all those cobwebs on the stuff you've been meaning to get to. Catch up on your horror reading and movie watching. Clean out unwanted horror items and donate them to an unfortunate horror addict who isn't able to afford them. Clean out your black eyeliners and mascara. It is recommended that you change out your mascara every 3 months. For the guys, wouldn't this be a great time to buy some new socks? The holes, just aren't working for us.

HORRORSCOPE: RAVEN
Be sure and fly above the drama when the proverbial feathers hit the fan. Just be sure not to perch on the wrong shoulder. When visiting authors late at night, please be courteous and bring libation before you go squawking and carrying on. A stiff drink will get you a long way and maybe even save your life.
To Do List
☐   1. Spring Horror clean out.
☐   2. Plan your Halloween costume. No, it's not too early.
☐   3. Pull out your Necronomicon, brush up on your Latin.
☐   4. Let your inner mad scientist play with a project.
☐   5. Visit a haunted insane asylum.
☐   6. Read some Irish horror stories.

MOVIE LIST

Leprechaun, 1993
Leprechaun 2, 3,4,5,6
Legend of the Bog, 2009

Donnie Darko, 2001
Maniac Cop, 1988
Grabbers, 2012

TRIVIA

☠   March 10th 1997 The TV series *Buffy the Vampire Slayer* premieres.

☠   The Broadway production of *Rocky Horror Picture Show* opened March 1975.

☠   Director Don Coscarelli dreamed the basic concept of *Phantasm* when he was a teenager.

HORROR DATES TO REMEMBER

1. Anthony Margo, *The Addams Family* 60's TV
2. Peter Straub, author
3. Jessica Biel, *The Texas Chainsaw Massacre*, 2003
4. Catherine O'Hara, *The Nightmare Before Christmas*, 1993
5. Dean Stockwell, *The Langoliers*, 1995
6. Allison Hayes, *The Zombies of Mora Tau*, 1957
7. Rachel Weisz, *The Mummy*, 1999
8. Kat Von D, *The Bleeding*, 2009
9. Gerald Brom, artist
10. Gina Philips, *Jeepers Creepers*, 2001
11. Elias Koteas, *Let Me In*, 2010
12. Takashi Shimura, *Godzilla*, 1954
13. Deborah Raffin, *Scanners II*, 1991
14. Mercedes McNab, *Buffy's* Harmony, 00's TV
15. David Cronenberg, dir. *Fly*, 1986
16. Gore Verbinski, dir. *The Ring*, 2002
17. Edward Gilbert White, *Natural Born Killers*, 1994
18. Brad Dourif, Chucky in *Child's Play Series*
19. Bruce Willis, *The Sixth Sense*, 1999
20. Bianca Lawson, *The Vampire Diaries*, 00's TV
21. Gary Oldman, *Bram Stoker's Dracula*, 1992
22. Andrew Lloyd Webber, composer, *Phantom of the Opera*
23. Joan Crawford, *Berserk*, 1967
24. Alyson Hanniganm, *Buffy the Vampire Slayer*, 90's TV
25. Bonnie Bedelia, *Needful Things*, 1993
26. Amy Smart, *The Butterfly Effect*, 2004
27. Quentin Tarantino, *From Dusk Till Dawn*, 1996
28. *Phantasm* released, 1979
29. Scott Wilson, *The Walking Dead*, 00's TV
30. Jason Dohring, Josef in *Moonlight*, 00's TV
31. Christopher Walken, *Sleepy Hollow*, 1999

APRIL

April for horror addicts starts with a bang, with April Fool's Day the first and then it kinda peters off into summer. All we can hope for is that April will be full of showers, making for excellent gloomy days and horror movie watching weather. Screw the flowers, April showers bring movie marathons! And for you little mad scientists out there, we have World Lab Day, so stock up on your test tubes and acids. Make sure to use your PPEE's! That's Personal Protective Evil Equipment for all you laymen out there.

HORRORSCOPE: GHOST

Although sometimes you feel invisible, remember that means people think you're not listening. Use that to your advantage and take notes. You never know when you can use your eavesdropping... I mean information innocently overheard, to your advantage. After all, being a ghost isn't always bad. Sometimes it allows you to hide from those you don't want to talk to.

To Do List
☐   1. Plan your epitaph. (6th)
☐   2. Appreciate your bat. (17th)
☐   3. Stock up on garlic (except for vampires). (19th)
☐   4. Stock your laboratory for World Lab Day (23rd)
☐   5. Tell a spooky story. (27th)
☐   6. Recycle, the spooky way.

MOVIE LIST

Spring Break Massacre, 2008   *The Evil Dead,* 1981
April Fool's Day, 1986   *April Apocalypse,* 2013
Easter Bunny, Kill! Kill! 2006   *Easter Sunday,* 2014

TRIVIA

☠   April 4th, World Rat Day.

☠   First week of April, "Be Kind to Spiders" week.

☠   April 5th, Qingming Festival, Chinese holiday to honor the dead.

☠   Arbor Day - Trees can be the scariest element of a horror movie.

☠   April 1819 The first vampire novel, *The Vampyre* by John Polidori is published.

HORROR DATES TO REMEMBER

1. Lon Chaney
2. Shawn Roberts, *Diary of the Dead*, 2007
3. Eddie Murphy, *Vampire in Brooklyn*, 1995
4. Anthony Perkins, *Psycho*, 1960
5. Robert Bloch, author of *Psycho*
6. Michael Rooker, *The Walking Dead*, 00's TV
7. Stan Winston, FX legend
8. Kane Hodder, Jason in *Friday the 13th*, 2001
9. Charles Baudelaire, spent years of his life translating Poe's work to French
10. Haley Joe Osment, *The Sixth Sense*, 1999
11. Jennifer Esposito, *Dracula 2000*, 2000
12. Tom Noonan, *House of the Devil*, 2009
13. Ron Perlman, *13 Sins*, 2014
14. Sarah Michelle Gellar, *The Grudge*, 2004
15. Glenn Shadix, *The Nightmare Before Christmas*, 1993
16. Lukas Haas, *Red Riding Hood*, 2011
17. Roddy Piper, *They Live*, 1988
18. James Woods, *Videodrome*, 1983
19. Tim Curry, *It*, 1990
20. Geraint Wyn Davies, Nick in *Forever Knight*, 90's TV
21. Robert Smith, The Cure
22. Jack Nicholson, *The Shining*, 1980
23. John Hannah, The Mummy
24. Robert Wiene dir. *The Cabinet of Dr. Caligari*, 1920
25. First execution by guillotine, 1792 highway man NicolasPelletier
26. Joan Chen, *Twin Peaks*, 90's TV
27. Matt Reeves, dir., *Let Me In*, 2010
28. Jessica Alba, *The Eye*, 2008
29. Michelle Pfeiffer, *What Lies Beneath*, 2000
30. Walpurgisnaught, Germany quoted in *Dracula*, 1931 as the night of evil.

MAY

The best we can say for May is it's only 5 months until Halloween. celebrate your gothiness by recognizing World Goth Day May 22nd in remembrance of goths that have been harmed because of their looks and to celebrate the freedom of being goth. May is also a great time to set off to those exotic locations you've been meaning to travel to like Transylvania, The Tower of London, or the Sedlec Ossuary where over 40,000 skeletons are artistically arranged to form decorations and furnishings.

HORRORSCOPE: SPIDER

You are great at spinning webs and connecting people, but beware of getting caught in your own trap. You may have eight legs, but be careful not to get pulled in too many directions.

To Do List
☐   1. Host an undead Prom.
☐   2. Hold a bonfire to symbolically burn all the negativity placed on you by the "norms".
☐   3. Celebrate your dark side.
☐   4. Have a Twilight Zone Marathon (11th)
☐   5. Set off for a spooky destination.
☐   6. Sing creepy songs as your take a midnight stroll down the beach.

MOVIE LIST

May, 2002

Mother's Day, 2010

Rosemary's Baby, 1968/2014

Memorial Valley Massacre, 1989

The Wicker Man, 2006

Prom Night, 2008

Carrie, 1976/2013

Wake Wood, 2010

TRIVIA

☠   Dante Alighieri was born this month. Exact date unknown.

☠   May 1st, Beltane Gaelic holiday. Light bonfires to keep evil spirits away.

☠   May 2nd, Paranormal Day

☠   May 11th, Twilight Zone Day

☠   Lemuria festival was held in May in ancient Rome. They preformed rites to exorcise malevolent ghosts from their homes.

HORROR DATES TO REMEMBER

1. Julie Benz, *Angel*, 00's TV
2. Ari Lehman, *ThanXgiving*, 2006
3. Kristin Lehman, *Poltergeist: The Legacy*, 90's TV
4. Emily Perkins, Brigitte in *Ginger Snaps*, 2000
5. Richard E. Grant, *The Corpse Bride*, 2005
6. Gaston Leroux, author of *Phantom of the Opera*, 1911
7. Traci Lords, *Blade*, 1998
8. Peter Benchley, author of *Jaws*
9. Kevin Peter Hall, *Predator* monster
10. Meg Foster, *They Live*, 1988
11. Salvador Dali, artist
12. Emilio Estevez, *Maximum Overdrive*, 1986
13. *Werewolf in London* released, 1935
14. Amber Tamblyn, *Blackout*, 2008
15. Katrin Cartlidge, Dark Annie in *From Hell*, 2001
16. David BoreanazI, 00's TV
17. Matthew McGlory, *House of 1000 Corpses*,
18. Priscilla Pointer, *Carrie*, 1976
19. Grace Jones, *Vamp*, 1986
20. Anthony Zerbe, *The Omega Man*, 1971
21. Fairuza Balk, *The Craft*, 1996
22. Cher, Witches of Eastwick, 1987
23. *The Shining* released 1980
24. Don Megowan, *Tales of Frankenstein*, 1958
25. Poppy Z. Brite, author
26. Peter Cushing, *Horror of Dracula*, 1958
27. Vincent Price / Christopher Lee
28. Zelda Rubinstein, *Poltergeist*, 1982
29. Danny Elfman, composer
30. Dennis Etchison, author of *Halloween*
31. Akira Ifukube, composer

June is probably the most hated time of the year for the horror addict because of the first day of summer. Black clothes don't do well in the sun. All the scarves and sweaters are truly put away and you have to start worrying about your eyeliner melting. Take heart, hopefully there'll be some good summer blockbusters to hide in. A cool movie theater is a great place to hide, if they can get our horror monsters right! June is also a great time to reconnect with friends. Chances are, they are just as miserable as you are. Invite them to an air-conditioned place for a cool drink and geek-out on horror stuff.

HORRORSCOPE: VAMPIRE

Whether you're the sexy kinda vamp or the scary kind, beware of sucking the wrong type of blood. Your hunger could be your undoing. As a vampire, you tend to overdo everything. Moderation while giving in to your passions will make you much happier in the long run.

To Do List

☐ 1. Dust out the closets, sweep all the little spider friends back outside.

☐ 2. Take a late evening walk while the temperature is lower and the moon is at its best viewing.

☐ 3. Hum... what other nighttime activities might you enjoy?

☐ 4. Get married horror style! Have the grim reaper officiate.

☐ 5. Honeymoon in Transylvania.

☐ 6. Go hunting for bats in your nearest cave.

MOVIE LIST

Beetlejuice, 1988

The Corpse Bride, 2005

Step Father, 2009

The Shining, 1980

I Know What You Did Last Summer, 1997

TRIVIA

☠ The first time Robert Englund tried on the Freddy glove, he cut himself.

☠ Over 500 gallons of fake blood were used during the filming of *A Nightmare on Elm Street*.

☠ *Kindred: The Embraced*, the 90's TV Series was based on the popular vampire role-playing game.

☠ When *Kindred: The Embraced* was cancelled, Showtime negotiated to revive the series, but the unfortunate death of Prince Julian (Mark Frankel) halted the effort.

HORROR DATES TO REMEMBER

1. Michael McDowell, author of *Beetlejuice*
2. Zachary Quinto, *American Horror Story*, 00's TV
3. Imogen Poots, *28 Weeks Later*, 2007
4. Angelina Jolie, *Maleficent*, 2014
5. Mark Wahlberg, *The Happening*, 2008
6. Robert Englund, Freddy Krueger
7. Liam Neeson, *The Haunting*, 1999
8. *Ghost Buster* released, 1984
9. Johnny Depp, *Sweeny Todd*, 2007
10. *Tales from the Crypt* airs, 1989
11. Gene Wilder, *Young Frankenstein*, 1974
12. *Rosemary's Baby* released, 1968
13. Mark Frankel, Julian in *Kindred: The Embraced* 90's TV
14. *The Stuff* released, 1985
15. Herschell Gordon Lewis, "Godfather of Gore"
16. John Franklin, *The Addams Family*, 60's TV
17. Last public guillotine
18. Carol Kane, *Addams Family Values*, 1993
19. Daria Nicolodi, co-writer of *Suspiria*, 1977
20. Nicole Kidman, *The Others*, 2001
21. Juliette Lewis, *From Dusk Till Dawn*, 1996
22. Bruce Campbell, *The Evil Dead*, 1981
23. Joss Whedon, creator of *Buffy, Angel*, 90's TV
24. Chris Sarandon, *Fright Night*, 1985
25. *The Omen* released 1976
26. Peter Lorre, *The Raven*, 1963
27. *Dark Shadows* airs 1966
28. John Cusak, *The Raven*, 2012
29. *War of the Worlds* released 2005
30. Vincent D'Onofrio, *The Cell*, 2000

JULY

July hot weather and cookouts aren't exactly the horror addicts favorite thing, but fireworks can be a great way to get a jolt and practice your apocalypse emergency drills. Try a drinking game with your friends. Every time you hear a firework go off, take a drink and then try to recite the Freddy's Coming for You rhyme. Or, create a zombie scavenger hunt. Every item should be a survival basic and at the locations, the members have to pretend like all the "norms" are zombies. They are in a way, aren't they?

HORRORSCOPE: MUMMY

You hold the wisdom of the old sands and many come to partake of your wisdom, but make sure all of your loose bandages are hidden. Some of those greedy little scarabs will pull, pull, pull until you're completely unraveled. Reevaluate your belongings often. As a mummy, you tend to collect more than you need. Don't let it collect dust in your pyramid when it could be sold and pay for a needed road trip!

To Do List
☐   1. Tell a spooky campfire story.
☐   2. Build a scarecrow (1st Sunday of the month)
☐   3. Howl at the moon for Moon Day (20th)
☐   4. Celebrate the freedom to watch, read, listen to horror!
☐   5. Make sure your "go" bag is stocked for the apocalypse.
☐   6. Time for a backyard movie marathon!

MOVIE LIST

Uncle Sam, 1996

Jaws, 1975

Cape Fear, 1991

2001 Maniacs, 2005

I Know What You Did Last Summer, 1997

Return of the Living Dead, 1985

And so the Darkness, 2010

TRIVIA

☠ July 18th, Day of Bad Omens

☠ July 22, 1933, first modern sighting of Loch Ness.

☠ July, 27, 1979, *The Amityville Horror* movie was released.

☠ Although evidence was overwhelming, Lizzie Borden was acquitted of killing her parents.

☠ No one knows who wrote the riddle, "Lizzie Borden took an axe..."

HORROR DATES TO REMEMBER

1. Dan Akroyd, *Ghostbusters*, 1984
2. Elisabeth Brooks, *The Howling*, 1981
3. Deborah Duchene, *Forever Knight*, 90's TV
4. Gina Loolbrigida, *The Hunchback of Notre Dame*, 1956
5. Warren Oates, *Thriller*, 60's TV
6. Janet Leigh, *Psycho*, 1960
7. Shelley Duvall, *The Shining*, 1980
8. Angelica Houston, *The Addams Family*, 1991
9. Ann Radcliffe, gothic author
10. Jerry Nelson, the voice of The Count on *Sesame Street*
11. Hugh B. Cave, author
12. Tod Browning, dir. *Dracula*, 1931
13. Stellan Skarsgard, *Exorcist: The Beginning*, 2004
14. Harry Dean Stanton, *Alien*, 1979
15. Larry Cohen, dir. *The Stuff*, 1985
16. *The Fly* premiered in theaters, 1958
17. Donald Sutherland, *Invasion of the Body Snatchers*, 1978
18. Vin Diesel, *Pitch Black*, 2000
19. Lizzie Borden
20. Jonathon Morris, *Vampire Journals*, 1997
21. Josh Harnett, *30 Days of Night*, 2007
22. James Whale, dir. *Frankenstein*, 1931
23. Terrence Zdunich writer, *The Devil's Carnival*, 2012
24. Anna Paquin, *True Blood*, 00's TV
25. Micheal C. Williams, *The Blair Witch Project,* 1999
26. Kate Beckinsale, *Underworld*, 2003
27. Johnathan Rhys Meyers, *Dracula*, 2013 TV
28. Bruce Abbott, *The Re-Animator*, 1985
29. Stephen Dorff, *Blade*, 1998
30. Carel Struycken, *The Addams Family*, 1991
31. Kim Newman, author

AUGUST

August brings the possibility of Halloween supplies at craft stores and with them, the feeling maybe we've made it over the hump. Homemade costumes should be thought of and started. This is Frankenstein month, so pull out your sewing supplies and stitch Dr. Frankenstein style. While inventing new creations, pull out those clothes that need some TLC. Holes should be darned, buttons reattached, and lace/trim added. While working, think of the things in your life that need stitching up. Fall is coming and you want to be whole. Are there friendships or emotional ties that need sewing up too?

HORRORSCOPE: FRANKENSTEIN'S MONSTER

Sure, you've been chewed up and spit out, but you still managed to sew yourself back together (or had friends do it for you). You might not be as smart as the next guy, but your strength can overwhelm even the toughest adversary. Just stay clear of open flame, and you'll be all right.

To Do List
☐   1. Create Frankie cupcakes.
☐   2. Sew a monster project.
☐   3. Forgive your flaws, celebrate them even.
☐   4. Practice fire safety.
☐   5. Build a horror object from scratch.
☐   6. Watch black and white horror movies on silent and make up the words with your friends.

MOVIE LIST

Mary Shelley's Frankenstein, 1994

Bride of Frankenstein, 1935

Frankenstein's Army, 2013

Young Frankenstein, 1974

Frankenstein, 1931

I, Frankenstein, 2014

Frankenstein, 2004

Stitches, 2012

TRIVIA

☠   *Frankenstein* was released at first anonymously and was written for a contest.

☠   Authors used to mark their writing with sewing pins, making pages look like they had stitches ripped out of them.

☠   Like many other authors, Lovecraft wasn't appreciated until after his death.

☠   Ray Bradbury's ancestor was sentenced to be hung for witchcraft.

☠   Lovecraft and Bradbury were fans of Poe.

HORROR DATES TO REMEMBER

1. Lon Chaney, Sr.
2. Butch Patrick, Eddie Munster, 60's TV
3. Carolyn Jones, Morticia Addams 60's TV
4. *White Zombie* released, 1932
5. Bob Clark, *Children Shouldn't Play with Dead Things*, 1973
6. M. Night Shyamalan, dir. *The Sixth Sense*, 1999
7. Elizabeth Bathory, The Blood Countess
8. Robert Siodmak, dir. *Son of Dracula*, 1943
9. Robert Shaw, *Jaws*, 1975
10. Antonio Banderas, *Interview with the Vampire*, 1994
11. Stuart Gordon, dir. *From Beyond*, 1986
12. Dan Curtis, writer, *Dark Shadows* 60's TV
13. Alfred Hitchcock
14. Sarah Brightman, *Phantom of the Opera* Musical
15. Natasha Henstridge, *Species*, 1995
16. Glenn Strange, *House of Frankenstein*, 1944
17. Robert DeNiro, *Hide and Seek*, 2005
18. Roman Polanski, dir. *Rosemary's Baby*, 1968
19. Angus Scrimm, *Phantasm* series
20. H. P. Lovecraft
21. Marie Blake, *The Addams Family*, 60's TV
22. Ray Bradbury
23. Ray Park, *Hellbinders*, 2009
24. Alex O'Loughlin, *Moonlight*, 00's TV
25. Tim Burton
26. Yvette Vickers, *Attack of the 50 Foot Woman*, 1958
27. Ira Levin, author of *Rosemary's Baby*
28. Johann Wolfwag von Goethe, early vampire writer, 1797
29. Michael Jackson, *Thriller*, 1983
30. Mary Shelley author of *Frankenstein*
31. Nene Thomas, artist

SEPTEMBER

As all the little ghouls and goblins prepare for school, this is your chance to stock up on cheesy horror school supplies. While folders and notebooks sport your favorite spooky cartoon characters, lunch boxes and pencil bags can be perfect to keep all your Halloween craft supplies in order. Halloween stores open this month and that means the blessed event is only a month away. Plan to get all your shopping done now, so you are ahead of the game. Stock up on the essential baking goods that pop into recipes unexpectedly like oil, baking powder, corn starch, and food coloring.

HORRORSCOPE: WEREWOLF

Sure, you're the one everyone wants now that the pesky vampires have become overplayed, but watch your ego, man. Remember, there can only be one alpha. Keep watch of the moon and feed your beast every once in awhile. Otherwise, you might wake up in a cage.

To Do List
☐ 1. Get back into the school mode and read a classic horror novel.
☐ 2. Talk like a pirate (19th)
☐ 3. Watch out for your head on Sept 2nd, Beheading Day.
☐ 4. Buy your candy now.
☐ 5. Order toys or non-food items online to hand out instead of sugar.
☐ 6. Write a horror story that takes place in school.

MOVIE LIST

Faculty, 1998
Teaching Mrs. Tingle, 1999
Pet Sematary, 1989
The Substitute, 2008

Flatliners, 1990
Urban Legend, 1998
The Expelled, 2013
The Final, 2010

TRIVIA

☠ Oktoberfest starts in September. Does this mean we can start early?

☠ Sept. 14th, National Pet Memorial Day

☠ Sept. 2nd, Beheading Day

☠ Stephen King almost always plays a cameo role in the movie adaptations of his books.

☠ Horace Walpole is credited with writing the first Gothic novel, *The Castle of Otranto*.

☠ Elvira began in Vegas as a show girl. Her horror hosting didn't start till the 80's.

HORROR DATES TO REMEMBER

1. Yvonne DeCarlo, Lily Munster, 60's TV
2. Keanu Reeves, *Constantine*, 2005
3. Mantan Moreland, *King of the Zombies*, 1941
4. Michael Benjamin
5. Michael Keaton, *Beetlejuice*, 1988
6. Max Schreck, *Nosferatu*, 1922
7. John Polidori / Dario Argento
8. David Arquette, *Scream*, 1996
9. Jeffery Combs, *Re-Animator,* 1985
10. Nancy A. Collins, author
11. Tiffany Shepis, Scream Queen
12. Charles L. Grant, author
13. Richard Kiel, *House of the Damned*, 1963
14. Andrew Lincoln, *The Walking Dead*, 00's TV
15. Jonathan Liebesman, dir. *Darkness Falls*, 2003
16. 1st article about the Bermuda Triangle published 1950 by EVW Jones
17. Elvira, Mistress of the Dark
18. *Hellraiser* released, 1987
19. Tainth Lee, author
20. Asia Argento, *Land of the Dead*, 2005
21. Stephen King, author
22. Brian Keene, author
23. Alex Proyas, dir. *Dark City*, 1998
24. Horace Walpole, author
25. Will Smith, *I Am Legend*, 2007
26. *Elvira's Movie Macabre* begins, 1981
27. Meatloaf, musician, Bat Out of Hell
28. Naomi Watts, *The Ring*, 2002
29. Ken Weatherwax, *The Addams Family* 60's TV
30. Eric Stoltz, *Prophecy*, 1995

nightshade's picks

Greetings addicts. As you know the best place to fulfill all your horror needs is by going to HorrorAddicts.net. We try to keep it updated with episodes of our podcast along with news on Music, Movies, TV, Books, Fashion, and anything else we addicts like to obsess about. But here are a few other places you might want to check out that keep the horror addicts in mind.

Horror Trivia/News:
Horrorsociety.com
Goblinhaus.com

Jewelry/Dolls/etc:
Bloodtouch.com
Eyescreamjewelry.com

Magazines:
Rue-morgue.com
Fangoria.com

Clothing:
HilarysVanity.com
Fright-rags.com

Horror Writers Assoc.:
Horror.org

Gothy Goodness:
Shadowmanor.com

Haunts/Haunters:
Hauntedhouses.com
Homehauntersassociation.com

Communities:
Vampirefreaks.com
Horrorbloggeralliance.blogspot.com

There you have it. Some of my favorite websites. Email us at horroraddicts@gmail.com and tell us yours. ♀

HorrorAddicts.net

nightshade on horroraddicts.net

It's time for a history lesson because HorrorAddicts.net does more than publish this book. HorrorAddicts.net started as a podcast in 2008. Emerian Rich wanted to start a podcast that focused on the horror lifestyle after her *Night's Knights* vampire podnovel ended. The point of the podcast was to show horror as a lifestyle and include a short horror story by a featured author, a movie review, and a featured band. It would also have news on fashion, movies and maybe a haunted location report or two.

With over 100 episodes and 10 seasons the HorrorAddicts.net podcast is still going strong. The site has grown since the early days, when it was just a podcast. They have quite a few projects going.

They have writer's challenges such as their annual writer's workshop contest for new authors. Everyone who enters receives critiques by published authors and the winner gets their story produced for the HorrorAddicts.net podcast. They also have the Wicked Women Writer's Challenge and The Masters of Macabre Contest, where contestants write and produce audio that fans vote on for best story.

HorrorAddicts.net has been involved in horror conventions, both online and in person. One of these conventions took place on Second Life, including readings from authors like Mark Eller, along with trivia, costume contests, and music by Scream Machine. The Horror Hostess, Emerian Rich, also did horror programming for BayCon, the largest SciFi, Fantasy, and Horror Writer's Convention in the San Francisco Bay Area.

HorrorAddicts.net became a publisher in 2012. They released two charity anthologies. *The Wickeds,* which featured women horror writers and *Horrible Disasters,* which featured horror stories set around historical natural disasters. *Horror Addicts Guide to Life* is their third publication and they plan for more anthologies in the future, so stay tuned.

The only bad thing I can say about the HorrorAddicts.net podcast is, Emerian has never let me be on it. I admit, I can be a little scary but she could at least let me host one episode. Yes, I would torture the featured author and I would break the featured band's instruments, but that doesn't make me a bad person. Maybe if everyone that reads this posts something in the HorrorAddicts.net Facebook group, she will let me host, or I could just take over the show. Anyway, keep listening because you never know what HorrorAddicts.net will have coming up next.

HorrorAddicts.net:

For horror addicts, *by* horror addicts.

Keep horror news coming by contributing and being part of our horror addict family.

Top 10 author interviews

by Sapphire Neal

All right horror addicts, do I have a special treat for you? Well, let me put it this way…would any woman make a deal with a crossroads demon to spend a night with the boys of *Supernatural*? If you don't know the answer to that question, then you my ex-friend are in the WRONG place.

In honor of our 100th episode of HorrorAddicts.net, I wadded through the years of 13 Questions to bring you MY Top 10 favorite interviews! Whether it be their insane sense of humor, their demonically seductive personalities, or just their undying passion for what they do, below you will find the 10 Masters and Mistresses that have left a mark on me—thankfully it wasn't a black spot! Phheeewww!—as well as my favorite snippet from their interview.

10. Kimberly Steele

"I feel that my pathetic, obsessive lurking around Emerian's fabulous site and community becomes slightly more legitimized because I've been asked to interview twice." You may have heard the rumors going around that Emerian and Kimberly hate each other. After you read what Steele had to say about the rumors you'll see what's going on. "She's my sister by a different mister, I love that chica. Emerian and I share Criss Angel. We get at each other, but it's really Criss that's to blame. He's a slut."

9. Shaunessy Ashdown

Shaunessy prefers the "monsters" that are "closest to reality." "Serial killers, jilted lovers that fly off the handle, the sort of baddies you find in thrillers like

Psycho or *Fatal Attraction*. It's fascinating to explore what turns a person evil…though in the supernatural realm, witches and ghosts really capture my imagination, maybe because they are the most real to me."

8. Patricia Santos Marcantonio

Patricia shared with us an excerpt of her novel *The Weeping Woman*. Not wanting to give away too much information, all I could get out of Patricia was a small description about the excerpt. "It's what I call my Mexican exorcism scene. A healer is removing a curse from a young girl. Pretty creepy. You'll never look at a snake the same way."

7. Crystal Connor

"My writing affects everything else. I write at night, so I really don't have that much of a social life; everyone I love lives normal lives and sleep during the night. The way you're supposed to haha. But the transition from punching a clock and being financially secure, to trying to carve out a life on the earnings of book sales has really shown me who my friends are. And luckily for me everyone who was around when I was spending money like there was no tomorrow are still with me today."

6. Rick Kitagawa

"Hands down, my favorite monster is probably the *Creature from the Black Lagoon* and other aquatic-based creatures. While the Gill Man is not the strongest or most terrifying of the bunch, he just looks so frickin' awesome. Actually, I'm working on (yet) another comic project that focuses on the Creature and other monsters, but puts them in day jobs and awkward social situations with each other. It's actually completely not scary at all (much more slice of life/emo stuff), but that just goes to show how much I like the Gill Man. I'm even willing to do a comic that's not even remotely creepy because I like him so much."

5. Jennifer Rahn

"I am a scientist, currently researching brain tumors. I did a stint in the biotech industry after my Msc (sic) in Pharmacology and then did my PhD in breast cancer, so I've got quite a wide range of experiences that I could use to build up a story environment. I think it all gave me a lot of background fodder for the first novel, and I have an idea for a scifi whodunit, so it probably will provide me with background again, but the nice thing about writing fantasy is that it doesn't necessarily have to be scientifically accurate!"

4. Joshua Heinrich

Josh's relaxed nature took hold and he began to joke around while explaining his story, "The Basement," to me. "It's a bit over 1700 words. Originally written in Times New Roman. 12 pt, I believe. In English. There's a basement involved. Okay, okay. I'll stop. It's a story I actually wrote a few years back. It sort of jumps into the story of a woman locked in a pitch black basement, sort of following her actions and inner narrative as things come into focus. I'm not sure I really want to give any more away before your listeners experience the story. I guess that's the problem with promoting stories with twists or that evolve into something else as the narrative goes along…it's hard to give a summary without spoiling the whole thing."

3. Shana Abé

"I watched hawks a lot. Eventually I could identify entire families. They're graceful and deadly, and one afternoon I was watching them slice through the air when I thought, 'Dragons! Aha!' Because although hawks are cool, dragons are even cooler. You can say whatever you want about dragons, create any mythology you want for them. They are purely products of our deepest, darkest imagination. "In fact, there's a scene in *The Deepest Night* in which Lora and Armand are discussing why they—their species—are so feared by humans. Armand says: 'Because dragons are the most formidable creatures of all. Because we exist at the fringes of their imaginations, nefarious, and bloodcurdling and never quite fully defined. We can be shaped however they wish, assigned any horrific trait they dare to invoke. We're the accumulation of all that they fear, most of all themselves.'"

2. Wicked Women Writers/Masters of Macabre

There really isn't a specific WWW or MMM that I enjoyed interviewing over the other. In fact, I found that it was the experience of doing a group interview of so many extraordinary authors that makes my WWW and MMM interviews some of my favorite!

And my favorite interview of all time is…dun…Dun…DUUUNNNNNNNNN

1. Emerian Rich

As the Horror Hostess that she is, I had to ask what actually got Emerian into the horror genre in the first place? "Horror and dark beauty inspire me to create, to live, to be. It sounds like a rather strange thing to say, that things usually involving death or terror inspire you, but I think it is the key to horror culture that outsiders will never really understand. I think it is a true test of the soul when someone is tortured or brought to the brink or death. There is a beauty when a character decides to accept the darkside or when they conquer it through personal strength. I am not a fan of mass murder or child abuse or terrorism in our real lives. However, I am a fan of the child or wife or soldier who battles through and shows that our human spirits can endure pain and still prevail."

To find these full interviews, go to <u>HorrorAddicts.net</u>

top 10 audio stories

by David Watson

This list proves that Emerian doesn't like me. It's almost impossible to go through all of the episodes of HorrorAddicts.net and pick out a top 10. I'm sure I left out plenty that I liked but this is what I came up with:

10. Season 1 Episode 3. "The Show" by Kirk Warrington. I like werewolves and I liked the concept behind this story.

9. Season 2 Episode 13. "Santa Claws" by Michele Rogers. Good Christmas tale. Lots of fun.

8. Season 4 Episode 33. "Wings of Revenge" by Laurel Anne Hill. Well told story and I like the bats in it.

7. Season 3 Episode 28 "The Butterfly Collector" by Kimberly Steele. I liked this one and that's all I'm saying. This one got me in trouble because I was listening to it at work. Listen to it and you'll see what I mean.

6. Season 2 Episode 15 "Night Crossing" by Mike Bennett. I liked the book this is from so much I just can't keep it off the list.

5. Season 5 Episode 54 "Hammersmith House" by Emerian Rich. I like the premise, I like the use of a historic event and I like stories told in diary entries.

4. Season 7 Episode 72 Mark Vale, "Inkubus." Great voice and great production values.

3. Season 7 Episode 83 Shaunessy Ashdown "Commencing Slaughter." Great audio production, good story that may keep you from ever eating meat again.

2. Ronda Carpenter WWW entry Season 5 "Lust: Barring Lilith." Great story with lots of sex and violence what more can you ask for.

1. Season 1 Episode 6 "Hunt Night" by Mark Eller. Before I was on staff this was the episode that made me think of the HorrorAddicts.net podcast as my favorite. Good story about demons.

top 10 podcast memories

by Emerian Rich

1. Season 1 Ep 8 Arlene's "Forever," we were trying to record in the Hell Hole Tavern cemetery in Second Life and Arlene kept getting her hair caught on the cemetery fence and walking around bald.

2. Season 2 Ep 15 Mike Bennett's introduction on our show of "Night Crossing," which was the intro to *Underwood and Flinch.*

3. Season 3 Ep 31 The first ever Wicked Women Writer's Challenge

4. Season 4 Ep 37 Rhonda's Sea Serpent rising out of the water to kill us all!

5. Season 5 Ep 51 & 52 Jez and Fang fight in *GothHaus.* Eyeliner Vs. Top Hat.

6. Season 6 Ep 71 Really a treat for me to interview Patterson Lundquist, the #1 Elvira Impersonator. Not only was it an honor, but we had a lot of fun chatting.

7. Season 7 Ep 84 Interviewing one of my favorite authors, Andrew Neiderman. I wouldn't say it was the fun-est because I was nervous as hell, but to be able to talk to an author that has changed your life is an experience I won't forget.

8. Season 8 No Episode I got to interview Mike Bennett live via Skype at BayCon and it was so awesome. The audio messed up and I was unable to share it with you, but those of us that were there were so thrilled. Definitely something we'll never forget. If you think Mike Bennett is cool on his podcasts, he is even more awesome live!

9. Season 1 Horror Con in Second Life. Was so much fun. We had free rein because Mark Eller was the host and he let me do whatever I wanted. We had poetry readings in the cemetery, he killed me in the tavern, and then we had a fashion show by hanging for Mimielle's fashion label in SL where I walked the cat walk, got hung, and then dropped down to make my final lap. Was so much fun!

10. I will never forget my very first show. I was fresh off my first ever podcast called Office Angst, I wanted to do something to do with Horror and I had no idea if this show would fly or even if it would go past that first episode. Sad thing is I think I've lost it... It was deleted from the site and I can't find it in my archive... so it might be lost forever!

the
addicts

Carmen Masloski – Cover Artist   yoh665.daportfolio.com

Her passion for art travels through her veins, since childhood. Love for art increases with age, knowing the progress of her work, by turning a hobby into a way of artistic expression, which we call today, "digital art". Her work is becoming increasingly popular, obtaining some collaboration with other artists, writers, bloggers, and many others, thus her artworks being featured in some European Digital Art Galleries.

Catt Dahman – Author   cattd.com

Catt is a native Texan, is a prolific horror writer with Severed Press and J Ellington Ashton. She writes extreme horror (splattergore), mainstream horror, has a crime series, several prehistoric thriller novels, a zombie series, and historical horror. With degrees in psychology from Texas A&M, she delves into the personalities of her characters and the depravity of the human mind. She has thirty-four novels available, appears in several anthologies, and four more pending. One of her biggest accomplishments, over thirty years of writing, is working in the area of splatter punk and extreme horror, an area that she was once told was out-of-reach because of her gender.

Chantal Boudreau – Author   chantellyb.wordpress.com

Chantal is an accountant by day and an author/illustrator during evenings and weekends, who lives by the ocean in beautiful Nova Scotia, Canada with her husband and two children. She writes and illustrates horror, dark fantasy and fantasy and along with her Fervor Series and her Masters and Renegades series, she has had many of her stories published in a variety of horror anthologies, online journals and magazines.

Chris Ringler – Author   grimringler.wordpress.com

Chris was raised in Linden, Michigan, a where he lived and attended school. He fell in love with writing as a teenager when he started writing short stories and began working on fanzines with friends. In 1999 *Back From Nothing*, a short story collection was published by University Editions. He's been published in *Bare Bone* and *Cthulhu Sex Magazine*, received Honorable Mention in *The Year's Best Fantasy and Horror* twice, was voted Best in Blood on HorrorAddicts.net, and has been working on his writing and art. Chris has written and published nine books which range from horror and dark fiction to fairy tales. Chris is a writer, artist, weirdo, and was the creator of many events in the Flint area such as the Flint Horror Convention.

Dan Shaurette – Author   danshaurette.com

Dan is a goth-geek, a writer, a foodie, and a horror addict. What else is there to know? Visit him at his homepage, if you dare.

David Watson ~ Editor / Author   theallnightlibrary.wordpress.com

David was born and raised in Silvis Illinois and is a life-long horror fan. He has a bachelor's degree in communications from Western Illinois University and currently lives in Milwaukee, Wisconsin with his wife, kids, and three cats. In his spare time he writes, goes for long walks, does yoga while listening to loud rock music, reads, and watches way to much TV.

Dean Farnell – Poet / Song Writer   reverbnation.com/deanfarnell

I write quirky songs and poetry, mainly paranormal/horror themed. I take the songs and poems as a bit of fun. The songs are recorded in one single take so are raw demos in affect but have still been played on over 600 various radio stations and podcasts all over the world. I currently have eight tracks in the TuneVibe Top 1000 Indie Chart top. Ten, including a number one record, which has been there for over a year. My song "Ghost On The Stairs" has a feature in the book *Rock & Roll Ghost Stories*. "Friday The 13th" has been played on BBC Radio. The songs are available on iTunes, Tesco, Amazon, and Songcast.

Eden Royce – Author   darkgeisha.wordpress.com

Eden is a writer and editor from Charleston, South Carolina whose great-aunt practiced root, a type of conjure magic. She now wishes she'd listened more closely. Eden is the horror submissions editor for Mocha Memoirs Press and a regular contributor to Graveyard Shift Sisters, a site dedicated to purging the Black female horror fan from the margins. She is also featured in Sumiko Saulson's book, *60 Black Women in Horror Writing.* Besides writing, her passions include roller-skating, listening to thunderstorms, and excellent sushi.

Emerian Rich – Author / Publisher   emzbox.com

Emerian is the author of the vampire book series, *Night's Knights.* Her most recent full length novel, *Artistic License,* is about a woman who inherits a house, where anything she paints on the walls, comes alive. She's been published in a handful of anthologies by publishers such as Dragon Moon Press, Hidden Thoughts Press, Hazardous Press, and White Wolf Press. Emerian is the podcast horror hostess of HorrorAddicts.net.

Garth von Buchholz – Author   vonbuchholz.com

Garth is an author of poetry, non-fiction, short fiction and drama who lives in Victoria, BC, Canada. He is also a photographer and digital media producer.

H.E. Roulo – Author   heroulo.com

Heather is a Pacific-Northwest author. She has been published in more than a dozen magazines, anthologies, and podcasts. Recent short stories have appeared in Nature and Fantasy's special Women Destroy Fantasy issue. *Plague Master* is the first book in her *Plague Masters Series.* In 2009 her science-fiction podcast novel Fractured Horizon was a Parsec Award Finalist and she received the Wicked Women Writers award from HorrorAddicts.net.

J. Malcolm Stewart – Author   about.me/jaymal

Jason is an author, journalist and media professional who lives in the San Francisco Bay Area. His full length suspense thriller *The Eyes of the Stars* is available on Amazon.com along with his non-fiction collection, *Look Back in Horror: A Personal History of Horror Film.*

James lives in western North Carolina with his wife and their two sons (they have a toddler and a teenager. . .and you think YOU know horror?!). James is the author of the novels *Midnight Rain*, *The Wicked*, *Animosity*, and *Ugly as Sin*, and the quiz-book *666 Hair-Raising Horror Movie Trivia Questions*.

Jeff was born on the day of the first manned moon landing and narrowly escaped being named Apollo, Armstrong, or Rocket. His father worked for NASA Ames at the time. His granddad on his mother's side was a sci fi fan whose library included autographed copies of Isaac Asimov's Foundation trilogy. Both men were strong, early influences—and in the high tech 21st Century, it's easy to stand with one foot in reality and the other in thriller novels. Jeff is the international bestselling author of *Plague Year*, *Interrupt*, and *The Frozen Sky*, hailed by Publishers Weekly as "Pulse pounding."

Jessica is an editor by day and a zombie-killer by night (at least in her books). Since the first time she watched *Night of the Living Dead*, she has been obsessed with zombies and often thinks of ways to survive the uprising. In addition to her nonfiction book, under the pen name Pembroke Sinclair, she has written YA novels about zombies and the tough teens who survive the apocalyptic world. She has also written nonfiction stories for *Serial Killer Magazine* and published a book about slasher films called *Life Lessons from Slasher Films*.

Kristin writes for her hometown newspaper, *The Cumberland County Reminder*, and has been writing non-fiction, speculative fiction, dark fantasy, paranormal, and horror for almost twenty years. Along with numerous sports articles, print essays, online reviews, and pen name fiction, Kristin's first eBook was published in 2005. She is a member of the New Jersey Authors Network, HorrorAddicts.net, and the Friends of the Mount Laurel Library. Kristin's first full-length work *The Vampire Family* has been re-released with Eternal Press; and her seven book sequel series *Fate and Fangs* is available now with Muse It Up Publishing.

Laurel Anne Hill – Author   laurelannehill.com

Laurel's award-winning novel, *Heroes Arise*, was released by KOMENAR Publishing in 2007. Over 25 of her short stories have been published, most recently in the anthologies *Fault Zone, How Beer Saved the World, Horrible Disasters,* and *Shanghai Steam. Shanghai Steam,* nominated for one of Canada's prestigious Aurora Awards in 2013, is now recommended by *Writing Fantasy & Science Fiction.* Laurel writes science fiction, fantasy, steampunk and horror. Every June she serves as Literary Stage Manager for the San Mateo County Fair. She is working on her next novel.

Lnoir – Artist

Lnoir is a 25 year old artist living in Arkansas. Her hobbies include dolls, video games and watching horror movies in the middle of the night with her cat, Chibi.

Loren Rhoads – Author   lorenrhoads.com

Loren is the co-author of *As Above, So Below,* author of *Wish You Were Here: Adventures in Cemetery Travel,* and editor of *The Haunted Mansion Project: Year Two.* She blogs about cemeteries as travel destinations at CemeteryTravel.com. Her science fiction trilogy *The Dangerous Type,* begins in 2015.

Mary Abshire – Author   mary-abshire.com

Mary lives in Indiana and is a lifetime lover of paranormal, science fiction, and fantasy. She writes Paranormal Romance and Urban Fantasy novels with vampires, demons, werewolves and other supernatural creatures. Dive into her books and find action, suspense, a dash of mystery and seductive men with passionate hearts.

Mimi A. Williams – Author   kwJustesen.com

Mimi was born and raised in Utah, she was the kind of kid whose mom had to come in and take the flashlight away so she would stop reading and go to sleep. She has always been an avid reader and writer. Years of Public Relations work kept her writing on the job. Then, when her third kid came along, she decided to try her hand at writing professionally. In 2003, Kim earned her MFA in Writing for Children and Young Adults at the prestigious Vermont College of Fine Arts, and the rest was history.

Mimielle – Author   gosu-rori.com

Mimielle is an Addict of Particular Sensibilities who embraces the Dark and Historically Gothic Aesthetic in many of her life's aspects. An Old-school Gothic Lolita 'of a certain age' she is fond of dressing carefully and elegantly and perfecting her makeup to throw her monthly Tea Salon, staying current with the latest runway and street fashion trends, and always on the lookout for new and beautiful techniques that can be corrupted for darkly beautiful purposes. Hostess and Local Style-maker, she breaks the rules only to re-write them weirder but always with impeccable taste.

Patricia Santos Marcantonio – Author   patriciasantosmarcantonio.com

Patricia comes from a family who loves to tell stories so she wasn't surprised she became a writer. She is the author of *The Ghost Sisters and the Girl in Hallway B, The Weeping Woman* and the award-winning children's book, *Red Ridin' in the Hood and Other Cuentos.* She has also won awards for her screenplays, short films and journalism, and is currently working on a graphic novel.

Ron Vitale – Author   ronvitale.com

Ron is the author of the *Cinderella's Secret Witch Diaries Series* who hopes that people stop looking to be saved by their Prince or Princess and find their own happily ever after.

Sandra Harris – Author   sandrafirstruleoffilmclubharris.wordpress.com

Sandra is a Dublin-based performance poet, novelist, film blogger, sex blogger, and short story writer. She has given more than 200 performances of her comedy sex-and-relationship poems in different venues around Dublin and Ireland. Her articles, short stories and poems have appeared in numerous publications. In August 2014, she won the "One Lovely Blog" award for her (lovely!) horror film review blog. She adores the horror genre in all its forms and will swap you anything you like for Hammer Horror or *Jaws* memorabilia. She would also be a great person to chat to about the differences between the Director's Cut and the Theatrical Cut of *The Wicker Man*.

Sapphire Neal – Author   sapphireneal.wordpress.com

Sapphire Neal was born in a small town in East Texas in 1990. It was her love of storytelling that bloomed into her passion for creative writing. Formerly the Blog Editor and Author Interviewer for HorrorAddicts.net, Sapphire has decided to continue her education and broaden her knowledge in the publishing field. She currently resides in the DFW metropolitan area while attending school.

Sparky Lee Anderson – Author   sparkyleegeek.wordpress.com

I have been writing for over 30 years, I received my first typewriter at 6 years old and I've been pounding out short stories, Non-Fiction, essays and poetry ever since, (although now I've upgraded to a computer.) I am currently a Blogger at sparkyleegeek.wordpress.com,where I've written about everything from politics to living with chronic Illness to humor. I have 2 other Blogs on Blogger & Bubblews. I also paint on the side. I currently reside in Bedford, Nova Scotia with my miniature Dachshund, Lucy. I hope to write a novel in the future.

Steven Rose Jr.– Author   faroutfantastic.blogspot.com

Steven is a freelance writer and artist. He published his first short fiction collection, *The Fool's Illusion*, in 2013 and is working on another that's due for release in Summer 2015. Besides horror and dark fantasy, Steven writes science fiction, movie reviews and computer technology articles. Several of his articles can be found at Examiner.com. The following are Steven's many other interests: treasure hunting for '60s and '70s pop cultural artifacts; jazz, rock and disco; video games; diet colas; history; mythology; Eastern meditation.

The Stoneslide Corrective   stoneslidecorrective.com

The Stoneslide Corrective is an online weekly that publishes fiction, satire, and humor. The Stoneslide Corrective No. 1, a print edition, appears April 2015. It is a division of Stoneslide Media LLC, which also puts out Stoneslide Books. Stoneslide Books publishes novels. The editorial team consists of Mark Boutin, Tia Creighton, Erica Gingerich, Samuel Holloway, Christopher Wachlin, and Jonathan Weisberg.

Sumiko Saulson – Author   sumikosaulson.com

Sumiko is a horror, sci-fi and dark fantasy writer. Her novels include *Solitude*, *Warmth*, and *Happiness and Other Diseases*. She is the author of the Young Adult horror novella series *The Moon Cried Blood*, and short story anthology *Things That Go Bump in My Head*. Born to African-American and Russian-Jewish parents, she is a native Californian, and has spent most of her adult life in the Bay Area. She is a horror blogger and journalist.

Willo Hausman – Director   gryphonpictures.com

Willo is a director of movies and stage productions. She is best known in film for her work on *House of Games* (1987), *Laurel Canyon* (2002), and *A Family Thing* (1996). For stage plays, her direction of the haunting tale, *A Christmas Carol* earned her much respect as a theatrical director. Up next she is working on *Grim*, a 3-part stage anthology, and *Frankenstein*. She is also working on a stage play about Diane Varsi, her mother who starred in *Peyton Place* and a feature film called *Clare*.

Nightshade was inspired by the comic by Emerian Rich, first appearing in the DarkLives 'zine, circa 2002. The most popular strip was about Nightshade's birthday present. "For my birthday, I wanted a Barbie, but I got a spider tattoo. So I wouldn't cry, mom got one too."

acknowledgments

HorrorAddicts.net would like to thank all the authors, artists, and editor for making this book possible.

We would also like to thank the listeners, readers, and donators of HorrorAddicts.net for your continued support throughout the years.

And last, but by no means least, we thank you Elvira, Vincent, Edgar, Mary, Bela, and so many more for inspiring us and filling our lives with constant enjoyment of all things dark and foreboding.

All movie, actor, horror icon facts were double checked against Wikipedia.com and IMDB.com.

HorrorAddicts.net

Do you love horror?
Want to hear a podcast created by
horror fanatics just like you?
Listen to HorrorAddicts.net.

Real horror reported by real horror fans.
We cover the news and reviews of horror:

☠movies	☠games	☠books
☠manga	☠anime	☠music
☠comics	☠locations	☠events
☠rpgs	☠fashion	☠more!

Every episode features horror authors, podcasters,
movie people, musicians, and horror personalities.

Featuring the annual Wicked Women Writer's
Challenge, Masters of Macabre Contest, and Writer's
Workshop Competition.

for Horror Addicts, *by* Horror Addicts.
Your one stop horror source:

HorrorAddicts.net

HorrorAddicts.net presents thirteen horror tales from up-and-coming women writers. This diverse collection of revenge, torture, and macabre is sure to quench any horror addict's thirst for blood. Between these covers reside werewolves, demons, ghosts, vampires, a voodoo priestess, headless horseman, Bloody Mary, and human monsters who are perhaps the most disturbing. All proceeds will be donated to LitWorld, a non-profit organization that uses the power of story to cultivate literacy leaders around the globe.

HORRIBLE DISASTERS

HorrorAddicts.net proudly presents, *Horrible Disasters*. Thirteen authors from around the globe share their visions of terror set during real natural disasters throughout history. Travel back in time to earth shattering events like the eruption of Mount Vesuvius in 79 A.D., the San Francisco earthquake of 1906, and the Winter of Terror avalanches, 1950. What supernatural events went unnoticed? What creatures caused such destruction without remorse? Stock your emergency kit, hunker in your bunker, and prepare for...*Horrible Disasters*. Proceeds go to help disaster relief globally by way of the Rescue Task Force.

Made in the USA
San Bernardino, CA
04 April 2015